THE EAST COAST FLOODS

By the same author
The Great Ouse: History of a River Navigation
The Great Level: A History of Drainage and Land Reclamation
in the Fens

THE EAST COAST FLOODS

Dorothy Summers

DAVID & CHARLES

Newton Abbot   London   North Pomfret (VT)

FOR ZOE

British Library Cataloguing in Publication Data

Summers, Dorothy
The East Coast Floods.
1. Floods – England
I. Title
942.6′085′5   GB1399.5.G7 S8
ISBN 0-7153-7456-7

Library of Congress Catalog Card Number: 78-62489

Printed in Great Britain
by Biddles Limited, Guildford, Surrey
for David & Charles (Publishers) Limited
Brunel House   Newton Abbot   Devon

Published in the United States of America
by David & Charles Inc
North Pomfret   Vermont 05053   USA

CONTENTS

'There is no enemy but the sea,' said Teithrin, '. . . against which your sword avails not.'

'The level of the sea,' said Teithrin, 'is materially altered.' 'The level of the sea!' exclaimed Seithenyn. 'Who ever heard of such a thing as altering the level of the sea?'

'That is the beauty of it,' said Seithenyn. 'Some parts of [the embankment] are rotten, and some parts of it are sound.'
'It is well,' said Elphin, 'that some parts are sound: it were better that all were so.'

Thomas Love Peacock, The Misfortunes of Elphin

Prologue:

THE EXTENT
OF THE DISASTER

On 31 January and 1 February 1953 a great storm surge, accompanied by gale force winds, swept out of the north, causing widespread flooding of coastal areas, and involving grievous loss of life and extensive damage to property. The piled-up waters of the North Sea, whipped by the northerly gales to huge tidal levels, smashed through the sea-wall defences in hundreds of places from Spurn Head to Kent, scattering like proverbial chaff before the wind thousands of tons of stone and concrete. The damage extended over 1,000 miles of coastline, and involved breaches in the defences at some 1,200 sites. In some places not a mile of sea-wall remained intact.

The human consequences of the flooding in eastern England were unprecedented, since a great development of coastal towns, in particular holiday resorts, had taken place since the last catastrophe of that magnitude. In total, 307 people lost their lives, and over 32,000 had to be evacuated from their homes. Whole communities were isolated.

There were material losses on a large scale; 24,000 houses were flooded and damaged, some beyond repair. Vast industrial complexes, notably along the Thames estuary, were badly affected; some factories were partly or completely out of production for several weeks. Twelve gasworks and many power stations suffered varying degrees of dislocation and damage. Water supplies were stopped, wells and underground water resources contaminated with salt, and sewerage services interrupted.

7

Hundreds of miles of roads, including 11 trunk roads, became impassable. More than 200 miles of railway were put out of action.

Agriculture too suffered heavily in the floods when 160,000 acres of agricultural land, the majority of these highly productive, were inundated with salt water. A further 3,000 acres at least were damaged by floodwater backing up the drains. Sand and debris were scattered everywhere. Little of this land produced a worthwhile crop in 1953, and much of it took from three to four years to restore to normal production. Extensive damage was done to farmhouses and buildings, stacks, machinery and fences. Livestock losses included cattle, sheep, pigs, horses and poultry, and altogether exceeded 46,000 head. For some farmers the floods meant the loss of entire herds and flocks, and the destruction of a lifetime's labour. 'The weekend of January 31st–February 1st,' commented the *Journal of the Ministry of Agriculture* in March 1953, 'will be remembered as marking one of the most serious farming disasters of the century.'

It was difficult to estimate overall losses, apart from the damage done to the actual defences; but the home secretary thought that, measured in terms of hard cash, they probably amounted to about £30 million. Subsequently a figure of £50 million was considered to be nearer the mark.

The North Sea storm surge of 1953 does not figure as an isolated event of a magnitude never previously surpassed, and therefore unlikely to be repeated in the future. Those able to profit from the lessons of past disasters – and past disasters had been many – could not have pleaded lack of warning.

Chapter 1

FORERUNNERS OF DISASTER

For centuries the east coast of England has been a battleground in the unceasing conflict between land and sea, therefore defence against the sea is a persistent theme running through the history of every east coast town and village. The problem is twofold, stemming on the one hand from the incoherent nature of the cliffs between Flamborough Head and the Isle of Thanet causing land to be eaten away by the sea; on the other from the fact that much of the east coast is low-lying. Hence two types of sea defence are necessary: the protection from erosion of lengths of coast above highest sea level, and the defence of low-lying coasts against tidal floods.

On the Holderness coast of Yorkshire, between Bridlington and the Humber, the wastage of the cliffs has been estimated at 2 miles (3·2km) since the Roman occupation. Many townships and villages have disappeared into the waves. From the Humber to the Wash the coast is low, flat and alluvial; the beach entirely sand, with no cliffs, rocks or shingle. Almost all the adjoining land is below high-water mark, and for centuries entire communities have lived in almost daily fear of extinction by the sea. During the past 600 years the Lincolnshire coastline has been forced relentlessly landward, although the incidence of erosion must have varied as the shape of the coastline changed. Between Mablethorpe and Skegness five medieval parish churches have been submerged. Along many parts of the Norfolk coast also there has been little intermission in the ravages of the sea.

Between Cromer and Happisburgh the coast is wasting rapidly. Since the Norman Conquest the villages of Keswick, Clare and Wimpwell have disappeared; several manors and portions of parishes have been swallowed up. Overstrand suffered disastrously in the Middle Ages and is still suffering. Perched on cliffs of vague, crumbling rock, several buildings have fallen into the sea; the original church was carried away early in the fourteenth century. Cromer itself was once an inland town, whilst Shipden, on the seaward side of Cromer, has gone.

In Suffolk the loss of land during historical times has been greater than on any other part of the English coast, with the possible exception of Holderness. Its low, submissive, fatally sandy cliffs have proved no match for the implacable sea which has made tremendous inroads, overwhelming countless places, notably Aldeburgh and Dunwich. Despite William Camden's optimistic comment in his *Britannia* of 1610 that the sea was 'favourable' to Aldeburgh, 'how spitefullsoever and malicious it is to other townes in this coast', the fact remains that the original Roman site is now a part of the North Sea. Of the Aldeburgh that was mapped during the reign of Elizabeth I, half the streets had been inundated and lost by the eighteenth century. But it is Dunwich, once steeped in medieval splendour, a thriving port, prosperous town, the seat of government of Sigebert, King of the East Angles, and of a bishopric, well known for its Mint, and, in the thirteenth century, boasting a fleet of eighty 'great ships', which has achieved extraordinary fame from its destruction by the sea. The modest cliffs on which it stood have been gradually eaten away. By the late sixteenth century the town was reduced to a quarter of its former size, and its decline since then has been inexorable. At Pakefield, too, erosion has always been serious, so much so that in the past Lowestoft Corporation expressed frequent fears that if erosion at Pakefield were not checked it might result in the southern part of the borough being completely outflanked by the sea.

It is a similar story in Essex and Kent. The coast from Colne Point to Shoeburyness, and along the Thames estuary, consists of a tract of low, flat alluvial land. On the south side of the Thames, from Sheerness to Reculver, are low clay cliffs. During the reign of Henry VIII the church at Reculver was sited at a considerable distance from the sea. In 1809 the sea had so far encroached that the church on top of the cliff had to be removed, and later the sea made a total wreck of the village which then existed. Minster, formerly in the middle of the Isle of Sheppy, is now situated on the coast.

The main problem rests with the tides. Their effects are unpredictable, especially so on the east coast, where they have silted up creeks whilst devouring and abandoning land at will. But though the tides may nibble and encroach twice a day, the flooding and possible destruction of a piece of coastline largely relates to the really tremendous storms, the exceptional events that become part of local – even national – history.

Since earliest times the history of the east coast of England has been frequently marked by serious storms and inundations. Some have been localised in their effects, hitting perhaps one specific section with particular force; others have struck at the entire coast between the Thames and Humber. There have been at least fifteen of the latter in the last 1,000 years; probably there have been more, but due to the scantiness of detail in the contemporary records it is not possible to say with absolute certainty. Apart from these the storm floods of a more or less violent nature which have affected some part of the east coast since AD 9, have been not less than fifty. Thus it would obviously be a serious error to regard the 1953 disaster as the sole occasion for hundreds of years, perhaps ever, on which a great storm surge, massive breaks in the coastal defences, and resultant floods have occurred – storm surge or tidal surge being the name given to the evil genius which has caused such widespread havoc on so many occasions in the past.

A study of past storm surges reveals no time pattern and no sequence. They occur at essentially irregular intervals. Indeed it is virtually impossible to assign a pattern to well-nigh unpredictable meteorological factors, or to impose on them a periodicity, at which such disasters may be expected to occur. Because of this very unpredictability all that could be certain in the past – and for that matter can be certain today – was the need to recognise the inevitability of recurring storm surges, though no one could tell exactly when, where or how they would strike. The need to keep the east coast defences in a continuous state of readiness to meet the threat should have needed no emphasis, but until fairly recently there seems to have been no major demand for large-scale protection on a systematic plan, even though tidal flooding has never been confined to a few spectacular occasions. Therefore the walls stretching from the Humber to the Thames, fronting the open sea and winding interminably round tidal creek and estuary, have been breached with monotonous regularity for centuries past, causing flood damage of varying degrees of intensity.

It is impossible to calculate in human and material terms the losses from tidal flooding suffered by the east coast communities during the last 1,000 years or so, but the records indicate that total losses must have been colossal. Flooding was not, of course, confined to the open coast; estuaries were also liable to inundation as the swollen tides travelled up the rivers. And along the east coast the tidal creeks, estuaries and rivers are numerous. They probe deep into the heart of the land, widening the possible area of devastation, with towns and villages liable to attack by the waters on flank and rear. Large death-rolls in round figures frequently appear in reports of early floods; in the tidal floods alone they are often assessed as 100,000. However, as the whole population of England at the time was perhaps no more than 3 or 4 million, such losses of life are obviously improbable. They must therefore, be taken merely as signifying a very large number as there was no contemporary means of taking an exact census. Naturally the numbers increased as the reports spread. Apart from this it was a dreary tale of damaged property, drowned livestock, and land going out of cultivation, sometimes permanently. The earliest chronicled flood, in AD 9, drowned many people. In AD 60 a storm flood ravaged the coasts of Britain and Gaul and in AD 245 many thousands of acres in Lincoln-shire were flooded by the sea, never to be recovered. Damaging floods occurred in the Humber about AD 530.

The period from the eleventh to the fifteenth century was exceptionally stormy in the North Sea, and a series of great tidal floods struck like the blows of a battering ram at the east coast. The series began in 1086, which disaster was followed by a much more serious one on 11 November 1099, when a violent storm at high tide flooded the coasts of Holland and England as far south as Kent. Throughout the twelfth and thirteenth centuries other storm-floods occurred. The Elizabethan chronicler Holinshed described how, in 1236, a great tide pounded at the each coast 'for several days with unabated fury, washing up the Ocean in such tremendous waves that the banks gave way, and the whole country lay completely exposed to its awful fury'. Shipping was damaged, trees uprooted, entire flocks of sheep and herds of cattle were drowned, houses destroyed and beaches swept away. The toll of human life was appalling. According to Holinshed 'in one village there were buried one hundred corpses in one day'.

During the fourteenth and fifteenth centuries tidal flooding seems to have gained added momentum. So great was the damage that frequently entire communities had their taxes remitted by the exchequer. William Dugdale records in his *History of Imbanking and Drayning* of 1662 that banks were constantly being breached 'through the violence of the winds, and the raging of the sea'. The Thames tidal frontages in particular gave constant cause for alarm, since the river overflowed them at regular intervals, laying waste vast acreages of pasture and meadowland. In 1320 the banks between London Bridge and Greenwich were in a complete state of collapse. In 1322 and again in 1324 great gaps were torn in the bank between Green-wich and Woolwich. In 1326 a serious breach occurred near Bermondsey. Between Stratford and Tilbury breaching was incessant, and the tidal defences were for the most part in a condition of endemic decay.

13

The collapse of the sea defences could be economically disastrous. In 1392, through inroads of the sea onto land belonging to St Osyth Abbey in Essex, the revenues of the monks were seriously diminished. At Southfleet 100 acres of their land were flooded to such a depth that they remained permanently under water. Other lands which had maintained considerable herds of livestock became incapable of maintaining anything. Another storm, which had dire effects along the whole of the east coast from the Humber to the Straits of Dover, occurred in 1570. Holinshed described how livestock losses were everywhere catastrophic. Near Grimsby 1,100 sheep were drowned. Their shepherd was 'found dead, standing upright in a ditch'. Also noteworthy is the 'dreadful inundation of the sea' which occurred on 1 November 1613. Norfolk Marshland in particular suffered appalling damage. At Terrington the collapse of the sea-banks was total and involved the town in enormous losses. An inventory drawn up at the time makes dismal reading: a bridge was shattered, over 2,000 head of livestock drowned, 480 acres of land sown with corn were swamped, hay and corn stored in barns was destroyed and 13 houses completely ruined. During the same storm the 3 mile (4·8km) long bank at Walpole was breached in twenty places, 'and the residue,' laments Dugdale, 'so rent and torn, as the making up and repairing . . . will cost a thousand pounds'. Walton and Walsoken suffered heavy losses. The town of Wisbech was singularly unfortunate in so far as not only did it have to contend with a direct frontal assault from the sea, but was also overwhelmed by water flowing from the Walsoken breaches. On this occasion the total losses suffered by Norfolk Marshland exceeded £37,000.

The remainder of the seventeenth, eighteenth and nineteenth centuries saw no diminution in the incidence of salt-water flooding along the east coast. Great tides still swept out of the north, gaining height and momentum on their journey south. In 1703 and 1736 there were unusually severe surges. That of February 1736 swamped the coastal lands from Lincolnshire to Kent, drowning thousands of cattle along with their owners who were attempting to save them. Some graziers lost entire herds. Foulness, off the Essex coast, was entirely under water; according to the *Gentleman's Magazine* of February 1736 'not a hoof was saved thereon, and the Inhabitants were taken from the upper Part of their Houses into Boats'. There were also exceptionally high tides in 1825, 1856 and 1881, whilst in 1897 there occurred one of the most destructive tides for which anything like full records are available. Banks round the marshes at Cley in Norfolk were broken and the Wiveton valley deeply flooded. One mile (1·6km) was detached from the tip of Orfordness shingle spit, and great damage was done by flooding and dyke-breaching in Essex, including Foulness and Canvcy Island. At the Horsey Gap in Norfolk the tide breached the sand dunes and caused serious flooding. New defences here were swept away in 1907 and again in 1938 when, on the night of 12 February, the high tide tore a 517yd (473m) gap in the dunes, causing sea-water floods covering 7,500 acres and extending 5 miles (8km) inland. Horsey Gap was fast becoming notorious, but the troubles were still not at an end. The repaired breach was carried away by a north-westerly gale in the following April. In 1928 and 1938 there had been extraordinarily high tides at numerous points along the east coast. The tide of Friday night, 6–7 January 1928, damaged the homes of thousands of London families when the Thames overflowed its embankments. Then, on 1 March 1949, strong westerly and north-westerly winds caused a storm surge, and the east coast took a tremendous battering. On length after length walls were cracked, crests damaged, backing material washed out, faces scarred, with even some breaching The 1949 storm underlined the warnings given on previous occasions. Again it was proved that the defences were too low and too weak.

In considering the causes, from earliest times certainly up to the close of the nineteenth century, of such a long catalogue of sea-flood disasters, it is not always possible to define which constituted the graver problem: neglect, ignorance, or sheer inability to maintain the defences in the teeth of adverse weather conditions.

15

So far as the defences were concerned local authorities and central government alike did have a clear appreciation of the need for adequate sea-walls to protect life and property from inroads of the sea. The endless floods served as a perpetual reminder. A sea-bank erected on the coast, on the farthest edge of the firm land, protected each town or village from the sea. Outside the wall, along many sections of the coast, lay salt marsh which was liable to be flooded at every spring tide. Deposits from the sea gradually accumulated on the marsh until it was left high and dry and ready to be enclosed for future cultivation. In course of time the enclosures grew in number, salt marsh became fresh marsh after about ten years and was amalgamated with the village lands by the construction of a new sea-bank. The old bank fell into decay. Along some parts of the coast accretions of salt marsh were comparatively rapid, so that the sea-banks were constantly being pushed outwards.

In most areas the battle to maintain the banks protecting valuable farmland from the ravages of the sea was incessant. Constant surveys were taken of the walls defending the Isles of Thanet and Sheppey and the Kent coast. In 1369 commissioners were appointed to supervise the fortification of the entire Isle of Thanet with banks and ditches. In the year 1385–6 comprehensive improvements were made to Kent's coastal embankments, and in 1388–9 the Thanet defences were again surveyed, heightened and strengthened. The struggle to keep the Thames tidal embankments in some semblance of repair was unremitting, whilst the coastline of Holland and Marshland bordering the Wash was defended by great earth banks, whose origin is often attributed to the Romans. In some places these were thatched to protect them from weathering and scour; in very exposed places the defences were constructed 'very strongly with lime and stone'. In 1324–5 large sections of the Holland embankments were raised 2ft (0·6m) higher and broadened by 12ft (3·7m). In Norfolk Marshland sea defence seems to have been carried to a comparatively advanced stage, so vulnerable was the region to attack from the sea. According to William Dugdale the inhabitants had systematically exterminated moles and rats which, by burrowing, undermined the walls. Every town was surrounded by a sea-bank called an 'indike' or 'ward-dike', in addition to the coastal embankments.

Thus each town assumed the aspect of a walled fortress, its population living virtually in a perpetual state of siege. William Camden, in his *Britannia*, described how the open coast of Lincolnshire also, exposed to the full fury of the North Sea, was 'fenced . . . against the Ocean . . . with mighty piles and huge bankes'. Nevertheless the local populace went in constant terror of their lives. They were 'faine to keep watch and ward continually, and hardly with all the bankes and dammes that they make against the waters, are able to defend themselves from the great violence and outrage thereof'. For no matter how much attention was being paid to problems of sea defence at this earlier period it would appear that the odds were heavily weighted against success.

In Lincolnshire the coastal embankments suffered perpetual mishaps, one of the most spectacular being the sinking of the Surfleet sea-wall into a quicksand, suddenly and without warning, three weeks after its construction in 1574: 'it was ordered that the same should be made again more substantially, and set upon a better and firmer foundation'. Occasionally really great efforts were made but found wanting. In 1594 extensive works were undertaken to protect the highly vulnerable Dagenham marshes from inundation. Unfortunately these proved unable to withstand the violent tides of September 1621, probably due, at least in part, to the absence of an adequate maintenance policy during the interim period – a common fault of much sea-defence practice. Huge breaches were torn in the Dagenham embankments, and it was necessary to call in the Dutch engineer, Cornelius Vermuyden, to undertake remedial works.

But it was the town of Terrington in Norfolk Marshland which furnished the classic example of the ineffectualness of seemingly impregnable defences against the force and impetus of the sea. Terrington, sited in an extremely exposed position –

17

William Dugdale called it 'a frontier town' – boasted the strongest sea-walls in the locality. It was 'very ingeniously fortified, not only with banks of extraordinary height and thickness; but with two mighty brick walls, armed and defended with piles of woodshoves, and other devices, of as much hope as the wit of man . . . could invent . . . within these xvi years, the said town had expended £20,000 upon the same'. But even these precautions, far-reaching as they undoubtedly were for that day and age, failed to obtain for Terrington immunity from attack. In the sea-flood disaster of 1613 Terrington, of all the towns in Norfolk Marshland, suffered the worst. The defences collapsed in ruins before the onslaught of the waves. It is to the undying credit of the people of Terrington that they did not despair in the teeth of this catastrophe. A new bank was raised nearer to the town 'by 600 acres' and 'in a place of better advantage'; it was 80ft (24·4m) broad at the base, 2 miles (3·2km) long, and 'with thickness and height proportionable'.

The 1613 calamity induced the authorities responsible in Norfolk Marshland to compile a number of general regulations which were designed to help prevent a repetition and were enforced with considerable rigour. The fact that they had to be drawn up at all suggests previous neglect, certainly in some quarters. All drains and channels were to be cleansed and deepened in an effort to facilitate the passage of floodwater. Responsibility for repair – an extremely vexed question – was more meticulously defined than hitherto. Every ditch less than 12ft (3·7m) from the back of the sea-bank was to be filled in, and in future no ditches or pits were to be dug at the back of the sea-banks within 12ft (3·7m) of the base. Hogs were banned from rooting on the banks, and sheep and cattle from trampling over them; a severe fine was levied on any owner who infringed this regulation.

But if strong, relatively well-maintained sea defences could not guarantee safety, the consequences of complete neglect were even more destructive. For we have seen only one side of the picture; there was another, more reprehensible, side. The complaint that sea defences were overflown or breached due to the neglect of those responsible for their maintenance is a theme which runs persistently through the drainage literature of the medieval and post-medieval periods. Even the Church, wealthy though it was, did not invariably give the lead that it might have done. In 1328 the landholders of the Isle of Thanet voiced bitter complaints because the sea-walls were 'decayed and worn down by the violence of the sea' due to the Archbishop of Canterbury's neglect. Some years later the Abbot of Ramsey was actually sued for damages caused by his failure to repair the sea defences protecting his land at Walsoken in Norfolk. Neglect could be endemic, catastrophic, even systematic. In some instances sea-banks were completely abandoned by those responsible for their upkeep, who argued that the cost of repairs far exceeded the value of the land to be defended.

Finance at this earlier period was organised on the basis that each man should contribute to the upkeep of the defences from which he derived benefit, in proportion to the extent of his land-holding or his rights in the reclaimed marshlands. Therefore the incessant encroachments of the sea not only involved the local inhabitants in heavy losses, but also in burdensome taxes for the repair of the walls. Taxes became heavier as the years passed. The burden was all the heavier for the layman to bear in that church land belonging, for example, to St Edmundsbury and Dereham abbeys, was completely exempt from taxation. Great lengths of sea-bank needed to be retained in repair. The innumerable creeks and estuaries complicated the problem, as banks had to be maintained up to the farthest limits of tidal penetration or influence. The towns of Norfolk Marshland were particularly vociferous in their complaints about the lengths of embankment they were compelled to maintain, the frequency of the breaches, and the resulting heavy losses they had to bear.

The principle of proportional contribution towards the upkeep of the sea defences carried its own built-in problems. It was not always easy to enforce and afforded endless scope for litigation. Tax dodging was everywhere rife. Many who were liable for repairs found some means to evade paying their assessment, forcing the authorities to have recourse to more draconian measures. Persistent defaulters had their names read out in church, were fined or, worse still, had their lands confiscated. In 1325 Norfolk Marshland, according to William Dugdale, was spending an average of £1,050 per annum on sea defence; he laconically added: 'a vast sum in those days'. Despite this expenditure 'no less than seven hundred acres of land in this country were utterly lost' during the course of one disaster or another.

The organisation of coastal defence proved difficult, and the mode adopted was hampered by inherent weaknesses of the worst sort. From 1258 up to fairly recent times Commissioners of Sewers exercised supervision, deriving their authority direct from the Crown. Commissions were issued for particular places and localities, and at irregular intervals, usually to deal with a specific crisis. They inquired by jury into the state of the embankments. Where works were found to be defective they ordered their repair and made provision for their future maintenance. Commissions had a tendency to become worn out after a period and were replaced by others as need arose. Hence there was no real continuity of effort and policy. In a word, sea defence was run on strictly parochial lines instead of being regarded from a broad viewpoint. A perennial criticism lodged against the Sewer Commissioners was that a Commission only took action when individual owners called attention to probable breaches in the banks, and even then they were not always prompt enough to carry out repairs before the sea had broken through.

These anomalies were not eradicated until fairly recent times; even the Land Drainage Act of 1861 failed to rationalise the situation. The Commissioners continued as practically independent bodies, who were not responsible to any central authority or to the owners of property within their area for the manner in which their duties were performed. They could not be called to account for negligence or even if they failed altogether to do the work for which they had been appointed. There was no systematic audit of their accounts. In many instances the areas under the jurisdiction of these bodies were ill-defined or not defined at all. It sometimes happened that the Commissioners' powers were not exercised over sections of the sea coast which were clearly within their area. They were hampered by their constitution from carrying out really substantial works, especially works arising from a sudden emergency, whilst the liabilities of owners to maintain works led to even greater discrepancies. Faced with a stark crisis the Commissioners and landowners concerned were often active enough, but by then the damage had been done. The system really broke down over the lack of adequate and comprehensive measures to prevent sea-flooding, as opposed to dealing with it once it had occurred.

This type of organisation proved the more disastrous because each surge seems to have been higher than the last, and the sea defences had to keep pace with a progressive rise of mean sea level relative to the land, which was taking place in the southern part of the North Sea basin. Perhaps it has been a fault in the past that the embankments have always been brought up to the level of the last great surge. Worse, the longer comparatively flood-free periods have tended to breed an attitude of complacency and inertia, leading to inevitable neglect and so to equally inevitable disaster. There seems to have been what may be termed a permanent efficiency lag in the condition of the defences protecting the east coast.

The cost of sea defence mounted inexorably with the increasing height of the walls. Meanwhile from about the close of the eighteenth century onwards, the needs of an expanding population coupled with the growth of towns made it increasingly clear that the continued salt-water flooding of so much highly productive land was not to be tolerated. Moreover it was not only the coastal farmers who now faced ruin. Valuable property was becoming involved as industry expanded in many areas, notably along the Thames estuary. Previous floods had posed an awful warning, so that the whole question of sea defence began to receive critical attention.

Chapter 2

AGENTS OF DISASTER

We have established that the 1953 disaster, far from constituting some rare catastrophe, was merely the latest example in a long series of breaches and floods due to storm or tidal surges which have afflicted the east coast of England from very early times. Storm surges are phenomena which occasionally cause the water levels at a coast to differ considerably from those given by tidal predictions. While it is true to say that the usual tidal oscillation of sea level round the English coasts is predictable for many years in advance with a very high degree of accuracy, it is subject to sudden and often large errors in prediction due to meteorological disturbances, which may occur almost at any time and totally without warning. A surge is mainly due to strong winds blowing forward the surface waters of the sea, the resulting motion being known as 'wind-drift'. It can have its origin in the vast chaos of wind and water of the northern Atlantic; less spectacularly it can be caused within the North Sea itself. Tidal surges of 2ft (0·6m) or so occur frequently in windy weather. Higher surges are invariably associated with storms originating in the Atlantic. Here under appropriate conditions of wind the germ of a rogue tide is born, or in other words a tide which can claim kinship with no established cycle, but which has a life and behavioural pattern uniquely its own. In the first instance a wave is generated which passes round the north of Scotland and down the North Sea. If circumstances are such that the crest of this wind wave coincides with a spring tide a very high surge can be produced. This is what happened on Saturday, 31 January 1953. The worst storm damage is always suffered when a

number of factors react in adverse combination; even the somewhat sparse records of the very early disasters make this point
clear. In the great storm surges of the past certain constituents
have always been present.

Surges occur at the full or new moon, because this is when
the tides are at spring and have their greatest range. They are
accompanied by violent winds which usually blow from the north
or north-west. The danger period is between September and
April. There is another factor. Gales are proverbially associated
with a low barometer, and when the barometer is low over any
part of the ocean the level of the water tends to rise there.
Variations in barometric pressure can only cause relatively minor
fluctuations in the height of the tides but, coming on top of a
spring tide already augmented by a north-west gale, even an
extra few inches may make all the difference between safety and
disaster.

Another important and disquieting fact influencing the effect
of storm surges is that mean sea level in the southern part of the
North Sea is still rising relative to the land. In the context of sea
floods there is no doubt whatever that changes in the relative
levels of land and sea are of fundamental importance. Much
evidence exists that there has been a rise in sea level since
Roman times. Submergence of Roman sites has been proved in
Essex, and it is estimated that the land surface in relation to sea
level in the Thames valley is now 15ft (4·6m) lower than it was
during the Roman occupation. Because of a general rise of sea
level the risk of flooding from the sea has appreciably increased
in the southern part of the North Sea during the last century or
so, so that the incidental piling up of the tide through meteorological causes, perhaps on average once in a generation, has
appalling implications.

In the absence of meteorological disturbances the tides at a
particular place depend only on the movements of the moon and
sun relative to the earth. As the earth turns, the waters of the
oceans rise and fall, alternately drawn towards the moon and
sun and then, as the attraction diminishes with distance, they are

released. The tides are semi-diurnal; that is, two rises and falls of the tide are experienced in any place in about twenty-five hours. During the lunar month the range of tide – the difference between the levels of high and low water – varies between the neap tides of half-moon when the range is at a minimum, and the spring tides of the full and the new moons when the range is high. At full and new moon the sun, moon and earth are very nearly in a straight line, the tide-producing effects of the sun reinforce those of the moon, and thus the range of tide is at a maximum. At the low neap tides of half-moon the pull of the moon is counteracted by that of the sun.

There is a further cycle, which has enormous significance so far as storm surges are concerned. The spring tides have their greatest range at the equinoxes, when night and day are equal, about 21 March and 23 September. It is then that the highest high tides and the lowest low tides of the year are experienced. In January and February the spring tides are increasing towards this value. The tide of 31 January 1953 was a full-moon spring tide, approaching the equinox, but by no means exceptional as regards predicted range. It was due to exceptional meteorological conditions that the tide rose many feet higher than predicted, these meteorological factors operating in two ways: through atmospheric pressure and through wind. During the great storm surge of 1703 Daniel Defoe had recorded how his barometer fell so low that he supposed 'the tube had been disturbed and handled by the children'. Such a spectacular fall would indeed indicate an unusually deep disturbance. A rapid fall of pressure causes a rise in sea level on average of about 1ft (0·3m) for a pressure fall of about 34 millibars below the mean. It is reasonable to assume that, in 1953, a deepening depression moving into the North Sea would have induced a rise of sea level of about 1ft (0·3m) due to this effect. The additional rise in level, which proved to be so disastrous, was caused by the high winds.

Surges, as already indicated, are generated when a deep depression moves north-east between Scotland and Iceland, or when a deep depression has moved over the North Sea and lies

over Scandinavia; they usually occur in conjunction with either
northerly or north-westerly winds over the greater part of the
North Sea. A north-westerly wind is the most effective in raising
the sea level along the east coast, for storm surges appear to
travel counter-clockwise round the North Sea. The water is
first deflected to the right and piled up against the north-east
Scottish coast, then it travels southwards, hugging the coast in
the form of a progressive wave. The extreme disturbance which
it generates builds up steadily as it moves further south until the
level of the entire North Sea is elevated, the wind effect being
accentuated at some places, notably King's Lynn. Here the local
funnel effect of the Wash operates adversely, and this is further
aggravated by the traction of the local winds over vast stretches
of shallow water. The Thames estuary is another area of special
vulnerability. In the past nearly all occasions of widespread
floods along the North Sea coast of Great Britain and the Low
Countries, which have been associated with high tides, have had
the simultaneous occurrence of northerly or north-westerly gales
in the North Sea. Studies in this connection have revealed that,
out of seventeen cases examined involving a large excess of actual
over predicted level, not one was related to winds from another
direction.

That the north wind has a tendency to increase the volume of
water moving southwards is especially notable on the high tide
when the tidal current is flowing south regardless of the action
of the wind. The water steadily accumulates, and the piling-up
of water is especially marked in the southern North Sea, where
its movement is blocked by the coast owing to the rapid
narrowing of the North Sea basin between East Anglia and
Holland towards the bottleneck of the Straits of Dover. The
stronger the wind and the longer it blows, the greater the
increase of water it will pile up and set in motion. And everywhere the effect of the surge on low-lying coastal areas will
depend on the time relationship between this wind-driven wave
and the ordinary tide. If the peak of a surge occurs near low
water it is harmless. When a rise of sea level of 10ft (3·0m)

above its mean value was recorded at Sheerness and Felixstowe on 7 April 1943, because the greatest rise occurred just after the time of low water and had much subsided by high water, there were no serious effects. Conversely, should the peak of a storm surge occur near high water, at a period of spring tides approaching the equinox, the combination may well be fraught with disaster. For example the peak of such a surge in January 1928 had only measured 5ft (1·5m) at Southend, but it happened within two hours of high water of spring tide with devastating results. The terrible threat implicit in this situation is that on some future occasion a surge of 11ft (3·4m) or more might be superimposed on high water at the equinoctial springs. If this happened the results would be catastrophic indeed.

That the North Sea basin, open to the Atlantic Ocean in the north and almost completely closed in the south save for the narrow Straits of Dover, is particularly susceptible to surges of meteorological origin is shown by the following statistics. Between the disastrous surge of 1897 and that of January 1953, similar disturbances were recorded round its shores in 1916, 1921, 1928, 1936, 1942, 1943 and 1949. From February 1820 to January 1953 the number of occasions on which the sea level rose to abnormal height shows an increasing frequency, which might possibly be accounted for by the rise in sea level relative to the land already referred to. The number of tides recorded as rising to 11ft (3·4m) above the adjusted datum for the period 1934–53 is 49, predominantly in November and March.

The events of January 1953 displayed all the classic symptoms associated with great sea floods. On Thursday, 29 January, there was a full moon, and the tides were at spring. During Friday, 30 January, the first harbinger of disaster, a large depression of enormous complexity, was deepening and travelling from the south of Iceland in an east–south-easterly direction. Its subsequent development and movement proved fatal. By midnight of 30/31 January the depression was due north of Scotland. During this initial stage the winds over the North Sea gradually increased in strength, reaching Force 6 in some areas.

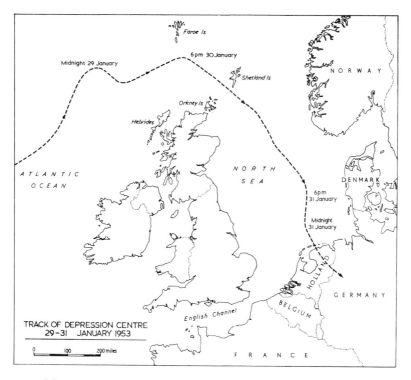

Map 1   Track of centre of depression, 29–31 January 1953

North-westerly gales had begun in the Hebrides during Friday night. During Saturday morning, 31 January, the winds reached Force 10 on the north-east coast of England and even greater force in north-east Scotland. Individual gusts with velocities of 113mph were recorded at Kinross on the southern coast of the Moray Firth. In the Orkneys a mean wind speed of about 90mph was recorded, with gusting up to 125mph. About noon, when the depression was at its greatest intensity, it swung south-wards into the North Sea and thereafter began to fill up. As it continued to move south-eastwards the rate of its advance accelerated to 29mph, and the winds following in its wake, circling counter-clockwise, were now striking the east coast of England from the north-west.

The extraordinary ferocity of the wind as it swept across the British Isles was reflected in the havoc it inflicted to shipping

27

and timber. The Stranraer to Larne ferry, the MV *Princess Victoria*, foundered in the storm during Saturday afternoon off County Down, Northern Ireland; of the 176 people on board there were only 44 survivors. A Fleetwood trawler sank with all hands south of Barra Head, and 28 per cent of the Scottish fishing fleet was lost. Inland in eastern Scotland the wind was violent enough to flatten thousands of acres of forest, especially in Aberdeenshire, Banffshire, Morayshire and Kincardineshire. Damage to the Scottish woodlands amounted almost to a national disaster. The timber blown down was principally coniferous and represented about 5 per cent of the total standing volume of softwood in the United Kingdom. Although most of the blown timber was salvaged, the all too meagre standing and growing reserve was depleted, and the loss affected forests and forestry in the region for several years to come. Never before had there been so many trees lying on the ground at one time in Scotland.

Meanwhile the pile-up of water by the gales had produced a sea of extreme danger to land areas as well as to shipping. The general effect of the north-westerly winds of record-breaking strength which had been blowing for so many hours, with an unusually long sea 'fetch' from the Arctic, had been to bank up the whole sea ahead and, as they swept on over the western and central parts of the North Sea on Saturday afternoon and evening with unabated fury, they drove the banked-up water south. But severe as was this heaping-up effect along the east coast of England it was even more serious on the coast of south Holland and Belgium. Tide and surge were partially reflected from the southern end of the North Sea, and in the ensuing northward movement the highest levels recorded were along the Dutch coast. It was later estimated that the prolonged and violent winds had forced some 15 billion cubic feet of water into the North Sea from the Norwegian shores of the Atlantic Ocean, raising its mean level by about 2ft (0·6m).

The maximum transport of water occurred during Saturday afternoon. Meanwhile the rapid fall in atmospheric pressure over the centre of the North Sea during the twelve hours between midnight on Friday and noon on Saturday had added its contribution to the rise in sea level. But this was not all. The general disturbance of the entire sea level was aggravated by the persistent fury of the winds striking the surface of the water and driving it against the east coast, to lash it in some places with waves reported to be more than 16ft (4·9m) high. These waves were steep and endowed with colossal strength on account of their great length and height. By raising sea level the surge made possible severe wave attack high up or even on the landward side of the coastal defences.

However, that the 1953 storm surge was associated with large and damaging waves was by no means remarkable. This had in fact been a characteristic feature of the great sea floods of the past. In 1953 certain conditions rendered it inevitable. The height of waves caused by wind depends on three factors: fetch, wind speed (strength), and wind duration. The fetch on this occasion was very long on account of the great length of sea track over which the north-westerly winds were blowing. Because the winds were excessively strong, long, high waves were generated. Some limit on wave size is normally set by the duration of the wind; on this occasion, however, it blew for about twenty to twenty-four hours. This meant that waves of more than 20ft (6·1m) from crest to trough could be expected, for example on exposed portions of the Lincolnshire and Norfolk coast.

An early symptom of the disturbance of sea level on the British coast was the poor ebb which followed high water on Saturday afternoon. The effect on the afternoon ebb was even more pronounced on the opposite side of the North Sea in the Netherlands and Belgium, where the strong winds, blowing directly on-shore, totally prevented the tide ebbing from the southern estuaries of the Netherlands. At Vlaardingen the record of the automatic tide-gauge showed no ebb at all after high water on Saturday afternoon.

In view of the very strong north-westerly winds a watch was being kept on the tide gauges at various stations along the east coast. It was by now realised that an abnormally high tide could be expected. The first indication of this had already occurred as far north as Aberdeen, and as the tide rose south of the border the disturbance began to assume a more alarming appearance. By 3.30pm water was pouring over the banks of the river Tees, although high water was not due for over an hour. By 4.45pm the water had exceeded its predicted level by more than 5ft (1·5m) and went on to rise a further 6in (0·2m). To make matters worse, by 6pm there was a long belt with a geostrophic wind of 140mph (120 knots) over the whole of the western and central parts of the North Sea. With the full weight of the gale behind it the situation steadily deteriorated as the surge moved south.

In order to be able to separate surge and tide, automatic tide-gauge records are essential. It was therefore a drawback of no mean proportions to later scientific study that such records for ports on the east coast of England during the 1953 surge were either incomplete or lacking. At all ports the sea rose above the highest levels which could be recorded automatically; some of the gauges were damaged, and others were rendered temporarily inoperative or were completely destroyed by the force of the sea. Consequently there were gaps in the records from the Tyne to the Wash, and between the Wash and Southend there were no records at all. At those ports where the gauges were inoperative the actual heights of the sea had to be estimated by interpolation.

Although the 1953 storm surge was very great indeed, it is difficult to assess what was really exceptional about it when compared with many other surges of the past; certainly not the widespread or prolonged nature of the inundation which had happened several times before. Neither was it the height of the surge for, although an examination of tidal conditions shows that the level of high water at many places along the east coast exceeded all previously recorded levels, the excess was not so great as one would have expected it to be, considering the extent of the disaster and the colossal amount of damage and destruction which occurred.

The magnitude of the vertical rise of the sea surface above its predicted level varied considerably along the east coast. In general it was greatest to the south, which was to be expected from the funnel-like shape of the North Sea. Therefore the sea defences most severely hammered were those between Holderness and the Isle of Thanet. It seems probable that the surge had an elevation of about 5ft (1·5m) at the Tyne; 7½ft (2.3m) at Immingham; 8ft (2·4m) all along the Norfolk coast, possibly reaching a maximum elevation of about 9ft (2·7m) in the vicinity of Lowestoft on the Suffolk coast; and then diminishing to about 8½ft (2·6m) at Harwich and 7ft (2·1m) at Dover. The lower elevation in the extreme southern part of the North Sea was attributable to the escape of water through the Straits of Dover. Levels were particularly high at King's Lynn, due to the already mentioned combination of large stretches of shallow water in the Wash and its geographical shape and orientation; here the elevation of the surge was 9¾ft (3·0m). Along the Dutch coast the situation was even worse. On the open coast the vertical rise of the water was 9ft (2·7m) on average, whilst in the narrowing channels of the inner Scheldt estuary, where the water was laterally constricted, it exceeded 10ft (3·0m).

It is illuminating to compare levels attained along the east coast of England in 1953 with the figures given for previous record levels. The heights at the entrances to the Tees and Humber only slightly exceeded those reached in December 1921. On the East Anglian coast the level reached at Great Yarmouth was less than a foot higher than that recorded in November 1897. The level of high water at Chatham exceeded by only 11in (0·3m) the previous highest recorded tides there of 1938 and 1949, whilst high water at Southend exceeded by 15in (0·4m) the previous highest tide of 1949. At Dover the level attained was just 1ft (0·3m) higher than the highest recorded tide there of 1943. As the devastation which occurred on these previous occasions was not to be compared with that of 1953 it seems permissible to wonder what had gone wrong.

There is another vital consideration – the state of the upper

31

rivers. In the upper tidal reaches of rivers such as the Humber and Thames the levels reached in 1953 were not so high as many previously recorded. At Goole, for example, the level was $1\frac{1}{2}$ft (0·6m) below that attained in February 1943. At Richmond the level was about $\frac{1}{2}$ft (0·6m) below that reached in January 1928. Fortunately there had been no prolonged period of heavy rain or melting snow in the uplands during the early part of 1953 hence, when the rivers encountered the risen tide, they were not swollen by land floods as they had been on many past occasions, notably in the Thames Estuary in 1928 – a circumstance not to be discounted in the future. Had this happened in 1953, especially if the Fenland rivers had been in flood at the time, the results would have been monstrous, in so far as, not only would flooding along the coast have been intensified, but it would have exerted its effects far inland, widening the area and scope of the disaster.

But the situation was bad enough as it was. And as the killer tide swept inexorably south along the east coast, sending off branches into creek and estuary, its accompanying waves pounding with terrible force at the shoreline, it became a matter of supreme importance to life and property that the defences should be in a fit condition to withstand at least some part of the onslaught.

Chapter 3

DAMNOSA HEREDITAS

The 1953 storm-surge emergency found the east coast defences and the authorities responsible for their design, construction and maintenance, totally unprepared. This state of affairs was not an occurrence without precedent, because the entire field of sea defence had for long been hopelessly bedevilled with weaknesses and problems. The sea defences as they existed in January 1953 represented the logical heirs, not simply of a short-term difficulty, but rather of a long heritage of partial neglect and consistent mismanagement. To illustrate this statement with sufficient clarity it is necessary to go back no further than the early part of the twentieth century.

In 1911 the Royal Commission on Coast Erosion had issued its Final Report. It had assembled a weighty body of material relating to numerous aspects of coast protection and had made many recommendations. Yet the impact of its findings on the country as a whole was insignificant. No immediate steps were taken to remedy the obvious weaknesses. Amongst the authorities concerned with sea defence there was still no general co-ordination of effort, and no appreciation of the value of research into the innumerable problems posed. It is doubtful whether there was even a partial understanding of some of the more outstanding difficulties requiring solution. Sea defence was organised on piecemeal and arbitrary lines. Prior to 1953 the major problems involved either went unappreciated or, worse still, were ignored.

Until the establishment of Catchment Boards under the Land Drainage Act of 1930 practically all sea-banks were under the control of various local authorities who, due to lack of financial and material resources, knowledge and foresight, did very little work on them. The Royal Commission on Coast Erosion had, in 1907, called for a more modern system of sea-defence administration to replace the outdated Commissioners of Sewers. The findings of the Royal Commission in this field can be summed up briefly in their own words: 'the whole system . . . is at present in a very experimental stage.' It may not be wholly inappropriate to replace the word 'experimental' with the word 'primitive'. Sea-defence administration was completely haphazard. The number of local authorities having powers and duties was by this time legion, and the powers under which they acted were very diverse. Besides Commissioners of Sewers appointed by the Crown, and elective drainage boards constituted under the Land Drainage Act of 1861, there were commissions appointed under the General Enclosure Acts or under Local Acts. Other local authorities having powers of one kind or another included certain harbour authorities, county and borough councils, and urban and rural district councils. In 1907 the head of the survey branch of the Board of Agriculture and Fisheries, when called upon to give the exact number of authorities responsible for comparatively short lengths of the east coast defences, was totally unable to do so.

The system was infested with more weaknesses than it is possible to enumerate. Commissioners of Sewers and local drainage boards, once appointed, were practically independent of everybody. The existence of many authorities tended to generate interminable conflict, the inevitable outcome of opposing interests. Not only were these bodies vested with widely differing constitutions and responsibilities; the areas under their jurisdiction frequently intersected and overlapped. There was no redress against inefficiency or neglect. In fact many of the authorities were under no precise obligation to execute sea-defence works at all. This meant that if such an authority failed to carry out work in this field there was no means of enforcement. Difficulties could be insuperable when a length of coast was divided between an urban district council and one or more rural district councils.

An urban district whose land was particularly valuable might execute expensive works. These could be rendered to a large extent futile by the neglect of the adjoining rural authorities, who might have no particular interest in the protection of the foreshore simply because they had no property within miles of the coast. Furthermore, of the 289 commissions of sewers, drainage embankment and conservancy authorities which were known to exist during the early part of the twentieth century it was not known how many were actively interested in sea defence. It was thought that the majority were not. There were many situations similar to that prevailing in Essex. Here well over half the tidal defences were not under the control of any kind of commission or board, and the twentieth century was to be well advanced before a move was made to establish responsible authorities in the neglected areas. Consequently there was a danger that long lengths of archaic sea-wall might 'give way at any time'. The defences were 'thin and altogether unsafe', 'in very bad condition' or breached outright, the gaps widening monthly as the tides flowed in and out. In April 1932 the engineer then in charge of the Essex sea-walls reported that 200 miles at least of the tidal defences were in an 'abandoned condition'. It was estimated that £176,000 would be needed to bring them up to an acceptable standard. The situation was just as bad, or worse, elsewhere.

The private ownership of many sections of the coast served to complicate matters. In the absence of an over-riding jurisdiction, individuals were constructing defence works to protect their own land. There was absolutely no coherence of activity. A private owner could erect on his own foreshore a structure which might damage land further along the coast. A central authority, or local authorities acting under a central authority, to control the erection of sea-defence works, and capable of taking a large view of the coast, seemed the answer to the problem. But the engineer W. H. Wheeler, author of *The Sea Coast* (1902), perceived no real need for local authorities in any shape or form, because 'each local authority would play for its own interest. I want something perfectly independent of local interest.' The problem of sea defence, he emphasised, was more involved than many people were prepared to admit: 'defence works ought to be undertaken with great discretion and by very skilled persons, who have in their minds the effect, not only at the immediate spot to be defended, but the effect beyond.' Doubts were expressed as to whether the bureaucratic machine, constituted as it was, and hampered by the often needlessly slow deliberations of boards and committees, was the best possible solution for handling so highly specialised a field of activity. It was feared that a great many non-technical members of councils and boards who had the task of deciding on the proposals of engineers were not fully conversant with all the problems involved.

Unfortunately administrative discrepancies were not fully corrected with the passage of time. In January 1953 local authorities, river boards, government departments, and even private individuals were responsible for sea-defence works which protected low-lying land from sea floods, whilst coast protection authorities, ie local councils, were concerned mainly with the defence of towns and villages situated on land above the highest sea level, and with the prevention of erosion. The fact remains that along the east coast, as late as January 1953, instead of one chain of command there were several.

In Lincolnshire local drainage boards had been responsible for strengthening and building defences until, in compliance with the Land Drainage and Coast Protection Acts of 1950, these duties devolved upon newly constituted river boards. Southwards along the coast the length of sea-bank between the junction of the Ouse–Nene catchment area and the mouth of the Great Ouse was 4 miles (6·5km), of which 2 miles (3·2km) were privately owned and maintained and 2 miles (3·2km) were constructed and maintained by the Norfolk Estuary Company.

On the eastern shore of the Wash the Norfolk Estuary Company's banks extended for a distance of 6 miles (9·7km) to a point west of the village of Wolferton. From this point northwards to New Hunstanton responsibility for the sea defences rested with the Great Ouse River Board, which had taken them over from the former North Norfolk Rivers Catchment Board on 1 April 1952. At Hunstanton itself there was unfortunately a gap in the sea defences between the river board's South Beach wall and the urban council's Promenade wall. The coastline from Hunstanton to Felixstowe extended for a distance of 116 miles (186·6km), of which 54 miles (87km) were the immediate responsibility of various urban and district councils, and boroughs such as those of Great Yarmouth and Aldeburgh; the rest were administered by the East Suffolk and Norfolk River Board, which also had 252 miles (405·5km) of embanked tidal rivers under its care.

The Essex and Kent River Boards, local authorities and the War Department shared responsibility for the Essex and Kent coastal and tidal defences. For example most of the coastline or tidal frontage from Woolwich to Birchington was under the control of the Kent River Board for both maintenance and improvement, but on certain short lengths, ie at Queenborough, Sheerness, Herne Bay and Margate, the local councils had an interest in the defences for amenity reasons. In such cases joint works had been undertaken.

In London and along the Thames the situation was one of even greater complexity than prevailed elsewhere. Along the river below the County of London, responsibility for flood defence was in the hands of the Essex and Kent River Boards. Within the County of London and the county boroughs of East and West Ham, the London County Council, West Ham County Borough Council, Commissioners of Sewers for East Ham and the Lea Conservancy Catchment Board had jurisdiction over the tidal defences. The Port of London Authority was responsible for carrying out protective work to over 30 miles (48·2km) of dock frontage. The local authorities along the remainder of the tidal Thames were the borough councils of Barnes, Brentford, Chiswick, Heston, Isleworth, Richmond and Twickenham. None was vested with the duty or power to execute flood prevention works. So the area was not conspicuous for notable tidal defences.

The *Final Report* of the Waverley Committee published in 1954 assumed, on somewhat dubious grounds, that past relations between the various authorities had been 'harmonious', but went on to suggest that 'owing to the lack of precise definition in the legislation, there is some uncertainty as to the responsibility of River Boards and coast protection authorities'. In fact, as the Waverley Report admitted, some localities were specifically excluded from the operations of coast protection authorities, whilst not being included in any area administered by a river board. In a word nobody was responsible; therefore nothing got done. Moreover the role of local authorities under the Coast Protection Act of 1950 was so imprecisely defined that a situation could exist like that at Hunstanton in Norfolk. Here a huge gap yawned in the sea defences, where a serious break-through of the sea was to occur, resulting in heavy loss of life. Conversely there were some areas under the statutory authority of both river board and coast protection authority. Here presumably were present all the drawbacks customarily associated with a dual command.

Neither did the financial arrangements enable much improvement to be made on this administrative chaos. Prior to 1930 the principle had remained firmly entrenched that drainage rates – and this included tidal defence – should be paid by those who benefited directly from any remedial works. A major defect of this particular system so far as it concerned sea defence was the comparative smallness of the areas from which rates could be levied because, in the absence of a general arrangement for levying a charge, only those lands immediately adjacent to the coast were affected. This made the burden of sea defence heavier than the lands and properties could support. The problem of raising money proved insuperable. There existed a sort of Alice in Wonderland situation where all concerned realised the need for putting the tidal embankments into some semblance of order, but where nobody wanted to foot the bill. In some areas the land was considered to be too poor to justify or support coastal defences. Eastington on the east coast of Yorkshire, for example, was financially quite incapable of maintaining its own sea-walls. The same principle applied along many parts of the Norfolk and Suffolk coast.

The expenses of sea defence were exceptionally heavy, especially where they fell on the shoulders of one individual. The sea had broken through the sand dunes several times at Heacham in Norfolk, and the local landowner, Mr Hamon le Strange, had been compelled to construct clay banks inside the dunes, together with a number of groynes, to protect his property. In the 48 years between 1858 and 1906 these works had cost over £16,000 and the expenditure for their upkeep had accounted for a further £6,000. At Corton near Lowestoft protection works on a substantial scale had been erected to defend the property of Mr Russell Colman from inroads of the sea. These consisted of a sea-wall and groynes. A portion of them was washed away in a heavy gale during the winter of 1907–8, and so much damage was done that the owner, despairing of ever being able to protect his property at a reasonable cost, had abandoned both the works and the struggle.

Although the idea was slowly gaining ground that responsibility for sea defence rested primarily on the nation at large, certainly before 1930 the attitude of the central government to the problem was casual in the extreme. Hence if a large project were contemplated and the rateable value of the lands concerned proved insufficient to bear the whole cost, the Treasury did not regard it as a matter of sufficient public interest to warrant a grant from central government funds. The Board of Trade granted small sums occasionally.

Because of rating problems it was virtually impossible to raise a substantial loan for sea-defence works. All the capital works undertaken had to be planned on the basis of loans spread over a long period of years. The amount of money which could be raised that way was regulated by the loan charges which the local authority concerned could safely meet from its revenues. Such a system engendered considerable problems, as was demonstrated by the situation at Pakefield in Suffolk.

There, erosion of the cliffs was very serious. During the early years of the twentieth century it was estimated that the cost of providing efficient protection would be somewhere in the region of £30,000. The assessable value of the parish was about £4,000 and the parish council already had outstanding loans amounting to about £3,900. It was obviously quite impossible for the parish, unassisted, to undertake adequate protective works.

However, the Land Drainage Act of 1930 should have represented a milestone, because under its provisions the upland counties were drawn firmly into the rating net. This made more money available for sea-defence purposes. Unfortunately, as a result of the de-rating of agricultural land much of the advantage was eroded by the agricultural uplands being exempt from making any contribution whatsoever. Even more important was the clause which empowered the Minister of Agriculture to make grants towards expenditure incurred in sea defence, amounting in exceptional cases to as much as 80 per cent of the cost of the works. From the financial standpoint matters had improved rather more than marginally. It is therefore surprising to find that there was still no evidence of any really dynamic effort being made to improve the east coast defences as a whole. Any work undertaken continued to be local, sporadic and of limited value in the vast majority of cases. Moreover there was no cessation in the complaints about lack of money; this has, in fact, always been a favourite argument of sea-defence engineers, when accounting for failure.

The 1951 *Heneage Report*, twenty years later, did in fact warn that river boards 'faced with substantial rises in costs without a comparable rise in their revenues, would be forced either to economize on their maintenance expenditure, or to defer capital schemes of new work and improvement'. Nevertheless some river boards had embarked on costly ventures, without achieving – as the events of late January–early February 1953 were to prove – the looked-for results. In this context the question of whether the greater problem was lack of money or lack of knowledge seems a pertinent one. There was a definite

40

tendency in many instances to fritter away money on basically irrelevant schemes, in large measure due to ignorance of the fundamental causes of sea-defence failure. Here the comment of W. H. Wheeler in his preface to *The Sea Coast*, published in 1902, is also particularly relevant to the later period: 'In no branch of engineering, perhaps, is there so little unanimity of opinion, or in which so much money is from time to time expended on works that are useless.'

The state of the Kent defences just prior to the 1953 surge provided an alarming, but by no means isolated, example of this type of uselessness. Here the defences were in the main reconstructions of, and adaptations to, existing works which had been found hopelessly inadequate in the past. 'Had it not been for the existence of the original works,' wrote the engineer in charge early in 1953, 'other forms of construction might well have been adopted.' He added: 'It is very seldom that complete new works are undertaken.' Other sections of the east coast were similarly handicapped.

Major criticisms of the sea-walls after the 1953 flood disaster were that their design in the past had proceeded by trial-and-error methods, and that they had been, in the main, a means of satisfying the exigencies of the moment – a rapidly thought-out expedient, very often executed in great haste after some disaster had occurred, thus making it difficult to give complete consideration to design. The implications of this were all the more serious because increasingly elaborate measures were needed to combat the menace of flooding due to the slowly rising sea level. If land were not to be continually sacrificed it was essential for the defences to be made increasingly stronger and higher, with the obvious implication that breaches would produce ever more serious results and floods become potentially more damaging. This long-term factor might have been expected to outweigh any misplaced optimism based on the supposedly low statistical frequency of storm surges combined with high tides.

Much of the blame for this wretched state of affairs must be attributed to lack of research, a point on which there was general agreement after the 1953 flood. Right up to that year, incredible as it may seem, there had been no continuous study of such general data as prevailing winds, depths of water, wave heights and lengths, the points from which the heaviest seas were experienced, and the set and velocity of the tidal currents as they applied to long stretches of coast. Yet a consideration of these factors was absolutely fundamental in determining the successful design of sea defences. Neither had a continuous record been kept of the changes taking place in the natural forces involved, even though any form of material improvement was hopeless until such records were available. Engineers could not start designing efficient sea-walls without having access to this sort of information. Local conditions, such as the presence or absence of deep water not too far off-shore, the growing out of promontories, and many other factors, including the operations on the flanks of other coast protection authorities, all produce complications.

Nor was it only research into methods of improving artificial defences which was virtually non-existent. Research into natural means of defence, such as seaboard vegetation and beach material, had been sparse. In the opinion of the Waverley Committee the behaviour and suitability of plants for use in consolidating sand, shingle and other material adjacent to the sea had not received anything like sufficient study.

But apart from the sea defences themselves, very little information was available on the generation of storm surges, coupled with their behaviour and possible frequency. With so many shortcomings it is not surprising that there was a considerable leeway to be made up in the improvement and maintenance of the defences when the 1953 storm surge struck the east coast.

Chapter 4

THE TIDAL DEFENCES
JANUARY 1953

In 1954 the chief engineer of the Great Ouse River Board claimed that during the twenty-five years previous to 1953 large sums of money had been spent on east coast sea defence, much of this in heightening the sea-walls and in converting earthen banks covered with grass into 'really sound modern sea defences'. The first part of his statement, relating to expenditure, has a greater ring of truth about it than the last. In fact the coastal defences between the Humber and the Thames estuary, whether of nature assisted by man, or entirely man-made, were either weak in themselves, or else weakened by the proximity of inadequate neighbours. The real purpose of sea-walls is, of course, to resist extreme tidal and wave conditions. The measure of their inadequacy in January 1953 lay in the fact that they were only effective – and that by a narrow margin – under strictly normal conditions. Where abnormalities occurred a point was reached beyond which the defences not only could not cope but virtually disintegrated.

Most of the engineers responsible for design, maintenance and improvement were anything but complacent about the state of the defences under their care, although almost on the eve of the flood, widely divergent views were expressed. The 1949 surge had clearly demonstrated the inadequacy of recent remedial operations; and had shown that the defences were too low and too weak. It is significant that some of the catchment boards concerned had so little faith in their defence systems that they had worked out detailed plans for military aid in the event of a sudden crisis. In a statement issued to the press in May 1950 the Essex board went so far as to admit that large sections of its own defences fell below the standard required to provide protection against exceptional but nevertheless recurring tides. Walls needed to be broader and higher. Neither was the board highly optimistic about future prospects; it was emphasised that 'in view of the immense financial and labour problems involved, they should make it plain that it must be some years before new standards can be established throughout their area'. Apart from this defeatist attitude, it was not reassuring to learn that the areas listed as especially vulnerable in the event of a break-through in Essex included the Bramble Island explosive works; Jaywick and Canvey Island, both heavily populated; the Dengie peninsula, important farming land; and the Thames-side industrial undertakings, valued at many millions of pounds.

On the face of it the situation in neighbouring Kent was more hopeful. Just prior to the 1953 flood the engineer in charge of the defences, in a published article, expressed the conviction that, whilst there remained lengths of coast where, under 'exceptional conditions', the risk of overtopping and damage had not been removed, 'the worst lengths' had been 'put in order'. Almost within days the Kent defences were smashed to pieces.

Even the turgid prose, congealed with lumps of official jargon, which comprised the *Waverley Report*, was unable to conceal the fact that much had been radically wrong. It was particularly unfortunate that the lessons of the 1949 surge had not been learnt. On that occasion a large number of breaches had occurred in broad daylight, and it had been possible to make a dispassionate and critical observation of many miles of affected embankments to assess the causes of failure. Although much of the 1953 flooding event took place at night, so that the evidences of weakness were in some respects circumstantial because actual breaching was not observed, the general consensus of opinion at the time was that identical tendencies had been apparent on both occasions. In a word the causes of failure had been noted in

1949; the same failures or types of failure occurred in 1953. It is surprising that so little progress in east coast defence works had been made in the interim. It is even more surprising that some of the weaknesses brought to light were elementary and might, with normal care, have been avoided or diminished.

The main general problems affecting the east coast in January 1953 fell into two broad categories, natural defences and artificial ones – first the natural defences: such cliffs as there were between Flamborough Head and the Thames estuary consisted almost entirely of glacial drift or alluvial deposit, and consequently were subject to constant erosion. Along the Lincolnshire coast there was no 'live' cliff, that at Cleethorpes – the only cliff between Holderness and Hunstanton – being protected by a promenade. The cliffs between Weybourne and Happisburgh in Norfolk are glacial. They vary somewhat in composition and near Sheringham and Cromer the stratification is confused and contorted; they are liable to severe erosion, particularly where silt and incoherent sands and gravels occur. The short lines of cliff along the Suffolk coast are all soft, of moderate height, and subject to erosion of a locally serious nature. In Essex the coastline between Harwich and Clacton is largely formed of low cliffs of London Clay, in height varying from 70ft (21·3m) near Frinton to less than 40ft (12·2m) in the vicinity of Clacton. These cliffs, far from forming a strong rampart, are subject to incessant denudation. Along the coastline of north Kent also there are areas of soft cliff which yield readily to wave attack. Damage to cliffs is, to some extent, caused through the hydraulic forces, engendered by the movement of great masses of water, but far more through the great quantities of gravel, sand, stones and rock which are hurled at the base of the cliffs by the waves. This causes undercutting, and blocks above are undermined and fall off; where there is a seaward dip of the rocks great masses may slide down the bedding planes.

In January 1953 costly defence works protected the towns and villages strung along the cliff tops. These defences usually took the form of heavy sea-walls with groynes designed to protect the quality of the beaches in front of the walls by preventing the erosion of beach material. Promenades were often provided behind the sea-walls, and in some instances additional protection was afforded at the back of the promenades by parapet walls or revetments, according to the dictates of local circumstances. In general the need to take account of seaside amenities had determined the design of the defences. For the most part the sea-walls protecting the cliffs, although in some places too low to resist wave attack above the ordinary height, were adequate. The 1953 surge caused a certain amount of structural damage to this type of defence work, but no great amount of flooding resulted.

Apart from the cliffs much of the land along the eastern seaboard of England lies well below the level of the higher tides. Therefore the effectiveness of the coastal barrier, whether of sand dunes, shingle ridges or sea-walls, is vital to the continued use and occupation of this valuable low-lying area. However, the maintenance of the natural sea defences, ie sand dunes, beaches and saltings, which should have been a first aim of the engineers concerned, had been neglected in many places.

In January 1953 long stretches of the coast between the Humber and the Wash, and in parts of Norfolk and Kent, consisted of sand dunes, in some areas standing alone and in others faced by concrete work or reinforced with a clay bank. Dunes are formed by sand blown up from the wide beaches exposed at low tide, and have a close inter-connection with plant growth. The common dune grass (marram) thrives best in those places where there is plenty of sand. The seeds take root on the higher parts of shingle ridges and, once the tuft of grass rises above ground level, it becomes a sand-trap. It is thus easy to see how the dunes grow. In some localities, where there is a wide sandy foreshore, new dune ridges grow up to seaward of the older dunes. But if the beach is narrow or steep and the amount of sand limited, the existing dunes are liable to severe erosion. This applies to much of the Lincolnshire coast between Mablethorpe and Skegness and to the Norfolk coast between Happisburgh and Winterton; the great breach made by the sea at Horsey in 1938 had been the result of the waves cutting through the narrow dune ridge in a storm.

Sand dunes are one of nature's main defences against the sea on low-lying coasts, and action can be taken to assist in their formation and preservation. Dunes are encouraged to grow by the judicious placing of brushwood and similar material to trap the blown sand. Stabilisation of the sand is assisted by establishing on the dunes various species of plant, of which marram grass is the most common. Certain trees and shrubs can also be used to consolidate natural defences. Since, up to 1953, the behaviour and suitability of plants for use on sand, shingle and other material adjacent to the sea had not received sufficient study in England, the sand dunes over several sections of the east coast were inadequately protected. Much more attention needed to be given to a long-term policy of dune conservation by wind breaks and vegetation. For sand dunes, although nature's defence against the sea, have several drawbacks, the more so if they are neglected. Dune vegetation seldom forms a close cover and the ridges can be readily destroyed. It is fatally easy for the wind to blow the sand away once a bare patch has been formed, perhaps as a result of a track worn across the dunes by pedestrian traffic. In Lincolnshire and Norfolk huge urban populations took caravan and hut holidays right in the sand-dune areas, consequently there was an incessant tramping about the dunes which reduced their height and vegetation. In some places there were huge gaps. When a flood occurred a great deal of damage could be expected from this human erosion. There was a real need to fence off the dunes where possible but, up to January 1953, this had not generally been done and the disturbance of the precarious dune rampart by trampling and devegetation was to have dire consequences.

But it was not only the sand dunes that had undergone dangerous depletion; in many places beaches too had suffered serious denudation, and this also was to constitute a major factor in the 1953 disaster. The width and height of a beach is important. A well maintained beach helps dissipate wave energy before it reaches the foreshore by increasing the distance of the wave break-point from the shore and greatly widening the surf zone. For this reason a coast lacking a naturally protective beach is inherently unstable, but in early 1953 beach level was so low over long stretches of coast that there was considerable still-water depth at high tides against the sea walls themselves, and heavy waves could break directly upon the defences. Under these conditions no system of sea defence could be expected to survive an exceptional emergency. The loss or damage of the dunes influenced this problem, for dunes and beaches are complementary in preserving one another.

Where the dunes had failed altogether, or appeared likely to fail, artificial defences had been built along some sections of the coast, taking the form of rigid concrete walls of various designs. Although these were the only expedient that could have been adopted having regard to the value of the interests at stake, rigid sea defences had proved in certain respects unsatisfactory, because they actually accelerated the erosion of beach material. The abrupt barrier presented by a wall to the advancing waves causes an undertow to develop which is stronger than that on the natural coastline, particularly with onshore winds. This readily scours material down the beach to expose the clay on the foreshore. Once this process has been established it is difficult to reverse, for the more powerful wave action in the deeper water actively erodes the clay itself, and this, once lost, is irreplaceable. Walls also hinder or prevent the natural reinforcement of dunes behind them, condemning the dunes to botanical degeneration and ultimate erosion by the wind.

But not only is the construction of walls generally disastrous to the beach in front. Unless care is taken to protect the beach the wall becomes the agent of its own destruction. As the beach sinks and the depth of water is increased, the volume and force of the waves becomes correspondingly greater. A wall not only has to withstand a heavier back pressure by reason of the greater depth in front, but also the footing is scoured away and the toe left exposed. The base of the wall is then liable to slide outwards, and the structure is in danger of collapsing in ruins.

The assistance which can be given to the formation of natural defences and to the protection of man-made ones is largely influenced by the amount of beach material which can be attracted to and induced to remain on the foreshore. The generally recognised means of stabilising the beach is by the provision of groynes, a system which, in early 1953, had not been everywhere adopted, or in some places had been wrongly adopted, or allowed to decay.

Results, of course, varied with locality, tidal currents, nature and drift of the beach and off-shore material, length, spacing and design of the groynes, and other factors. Furthermore, there was a recognised problem in that the effective concentration of beach material by groynes in one place could result in depriving the foreshore further along the coast. For example, a local land-owner near Sheringham in Norfolk had, some years previously, constructed a groyne to arrest the movement of beach material which was undermining the cliffs bordering his property. So far as he was concerned the groyne was a huge success, but it had dire effects at Sheringham a short distance along the coast. Considerably more investigation was needed relative to the movements of beach material and associated problems.

Along many lengths of the east coast, due to the lowering of beach level in front of the concrete defences, there was need of an adequate groyne system. The groynes that had been recently established along the Lincolnshire coast did not represent a totally unqualified asset, being only about 450ft (137m) long and a $\frac{1}{4}$ mile (0·4km) from low-water mark spring tides. Beyond the influence of the groynes the beach continued to erode; as it eroded it steepened, and as it steepened it would in time have an adverse effect on that part of the beach protected by the groyne system. Ultimately the defences would be overwhelmed.

In addition to sand dunes and beach, saltings, prevalent along many sections of the east coast, represented another essential link in the natural defence system. It was vitally important to preserve those situated in front of sea-walls. Relatively wide saltings afforded protection by reducing the number of times the base of the wall was washed by the tide. They also diminished the effects of attrition by reducing the depth of water which approached the wall. But in several places, notably along the Humber, Thames and Medway estuaries, the saltings had been allowed to deteriorate, and hence represented yet another item for inclusion on the list of squandered assets.

But if the natural defence system was not outstanding for its efficiency, the artificial system of protection for the east coast in January 1953 was even less so. Here the commonest form of protection was the earth bank. There were about 1,200 miles (1,931km) of these banks along the east coast, and about 70 miles (113km) of other types of artificial structure, fronting the sea shore or estuaries. The materials which composed the earth banks varied according to what was available in the locality, but usually they were formed of some kind of clay. They were generally about 4–6ft (1·2–1·8m) wide at the top, grassed at the top and back and, in unexposed places, on the front also. Where the banks were subject to direct wave action the seaward side was usually protected by a revetment of stone, concrete blocks, or other suitable material. This type of sea defence work was hampered by many weaknesses, and it was deplorable that residential and highly industrialised areas were protected by not much more than clay embankments, with crests too easily eroded when over-topped by storm waves.

In January 1953 long sections of the east coast were protected by embankments, many of great age, the majority neither suitable nor adequate for the sites which they occupied. There were cracks in the concrete and stone sea-defence walls in some places. Insufficient attention had been paid to stability. There had been a tendency to concentrate on protecting the seaward face and to neglect the crest and back face. Maintenance work had sometimes been slipshod. There were instances where a clay face had been superimposed on a body of inferior material. In other cases the reverse applied; old, well consolidated clay banks had been thickened and heightened by adding inferior

50

material, without any attempt being made to key the two together to form a uniform structure. Lengths of concrete walls which were backed by old dunes depended on sand-filling for support. This filling was inadequate in most places and liable to be washed out in a storm of any severity. With clay banks a major problem was that of seepage. This, combined with any overtopping which occurred, rapidly caused failure of the back. Although some of these banks were revetted with concrete blockwork the top level of the revetment had been kept down for economy reasons to the zone affected by the spring tides. To cope with extraordinary tides, impermeable revetment should have been carried right up to the top of the walls. In the majority of cases blockwork stopped within 2ft (0·6m) of the wall crest, and was of no value because the wave action rose well above it.

In general the sea-walls had no adequate safety margin. Only infrequently did they rise to more than 3ft (0·9m) above ordinary high-tide level. Many of the defences were lower than one and two-thirds of the height of still-water above the beach; the height of the waves was superimposed on this. Moreover the task of raising a clay wall was beset by difficulties. The problem was to devise a means of giving additional height without adding appreciably to the weight of the structure. Many of the walls were built on marshland, for example along the Essex and Kent coasts, where the subsoil was very unstable. To reach anything substantial, like chalk or gravel, it had been necessary to go down 100ft (30·5m) or more. Under these conditions settlement of the walls was a continuous process – slow, but in course of time appreciable. It could be as much as ¾in (1·9cm) per year. As the walls settled they were in constant need of replenishment with fresh material to maintain their proper crest levels. In the teeth of these hazards it was essential to devise a type of sea defence that could more easily be maintained at its required height.

But these were not the sole problems connected with raising and strengthening the sea defences. The *Waverley Report* had noted what it termed the 'sporadic and ill-considered development' near the coast. In many places bungalows, beach huts and other buildings had been constructed in pre-1953 decades in vulnerable positions at low levels close to the sea. Apart from the obvious danger to human life inherent in this situation, the presence of these buildings frequently prevented any effective works from being carried out to build up a proper defence line. In other localities extensive industrial undertakings caused obstructions. It was impossible to heighten the sea-walls simply because there was not sufficient room to widen their bases in proportion, without interfering with buildings, quaysides and other vital installations.

Due in some measure to the difficulties of widening, the slope of the sea-walls was often far too steep. A flatter slope was desirable, because it allowed the wave to break on the wall itself. This was particularly important at high tide when erosion of the toe mostly took place. The flatter the slope the more remote is the sand at the toe from the intense turbulence caused by the breaking wave. The usually accepted theory is that the gradient of the seaward and landward slopes should never be greater than 1:3 and 1:2 respectively. Not only is the wave action less severe but the longer slope helps to prevent over-topping with the consequent 'washing-out' of earthen material from the back slope of the wall. In January 1953 long lengths of tidal defences were more or less vertical, and hence vulnerable to heavy wave attack. In these circumstances it was doubly unfortunate that the earthen banks, which in many localities comprised second lines of defence behind the first-line defences, had been allowed to fall into disrepair, been ploughed down, or otherwise removed. They would have constituted a valuable asset in limiting the extent of the flooding.

Starting at the north of our area the main specific weaknesses in the defences on the eve of the 1953 storm may be briefly enumerated. Along the south bank of the Humber, between South Ferriby and Grimsby, there were 19 miles (30·5km) of tidal embankment. Eight miles (13km) of these consisted of a small bank, faced by saltings – an enormous advantage had the saltings been in good condition. Unfortunately they had been allowed to deteriorate. The remainder of the Humber defences, between East Halton and Grimsby, were well-consolidated banks of much stouter construction, which had been thickened and heightened by the addition of inferior material. No attempt had been made to key the two together. Several important factories were protected by this faulty wall. From Grimsby to Tetney Haven, a distance of $2\frac{1}{2}$ miles (4km), the sea defences consisted of sand dunes and a completely inadequate clay bank, neither high enough nor wide enough. Fortunately there was a wide foreshore along this length of coast, whilst Spurn Head afforded some shelter from the full force of the waves. The $10\frac{1}{2}$ miles (17km) of coastal defences between Tetney Haven and Saltfleet Haven comprised sand hills and a clay bank, which itself was sometimes buried in the sand hills. The foreshore along this frontage was about 2 miles (3·2km) wide and the tide rarely reached the embankments. As so wide a foreshore would break much of the force of even the most vicious wave attack, and taking account of the colossal damage that was to occur on this frontage, the weakness of the defences at this point must have been spectacular.

Between Mablethorpe and Skegness, southwards along the open coast of Lincolnshire, there was but a single line of dunes and a comparatively narrow beach. This was in direct contrast to the lengths of coast north and south of these towns, where the dune system was more complex and the beach wider. Significantly it was between Mablethorpe and Skegness that the worst flooding along the Lincolnshire coast took place. The dune barrier here was tenuous, and matters were not helped by the recent crowding of settlements and population on the low-level ground immediately behind the dunes. Even the dunes themselves were infested with camps, so that considerable lengths were in bad condition caused by the public trampling them down. At those points subjected to heavy pedestrian traffic not only were the dunes very thin but almost denuded of vegetation;

they were even non-existent in some places. In fact between Mablethorpe and Skegness there were but a few dunes left which might be regarded as adequate for sea defence. Nevertheless this faulty narrow dune line, apart from places where it was artificially strengthened by sea-walls, constituted the sole protection of the low-lying lands along this section of the coast.

The concrete erections that had been constructed in front of the existing dune system, as in some of the holiday areas or to repair breaches in the dunes which had occurred from time to time, were of varying types. When these defences were built it was thought that they were sufficient to hold normal tides, and so most of them were. But none were sufficient to withstand the conditions of January 1953. They were not high enough and the construction of some was faulty. Where the wall was not backed by a higher area of dune the sea could overflow onto the land, from which it could not flow back when the tide ebbed unless there was an outright breach. Walls of the type common at Mablethorpe and Sutton were unreliable because they were backed only by material which was easily eroded by overtopping water. The unsupported concrete was too weak to resist the wave pressure from seaward and the whole structure collapsed.

At the southern end of this district, between Sutton and Sandilands, was the notorious Acre Gap – no misnomer, for here the land was open to the sea for a distance of $\frac{1}{4}$ mile (0·4km), protected by nothing more substantial than timber piling. Precipitous sand dunes faced with concrete steps, and a narrow top deck occupied by a number of beach chalets, defended the extreme south of Sandilands. Behind the dunes was a narrow road and a number of houses. This arrangement fell far short of even basic requirements. The concrete stepwork consisted merely of separate masses of concrete laid on the sand dunes, and the steps were not reinforced or connected to each other by any adequate means. Therefore it was to be expected that if a moderately heavy sea washed over these steps the sand behind and under them would be quickly washed away, allowing the concrete, deprived of any support, to fall and disintegrate.

Further south the coast from Sandilands to Chapel Point was protected for most of the distance by two earthen embankments, one behind the other. The seaward bank was covered for the most part with sand dunes and behind it, giving extra protection, was a second earth embankment known as the Roman Bank. This was an important feature of the sea defences along this part of the Lincolnshire coast.

An extensive scheme of new construction, rehabilitation of existing defences, and groyning work had been completed during the five years up to 1949 between Trusthorpe and Ingoldmells, at a total cost of £338,000. This had included the construction of forty-four new groynes. Reconstructed stepwork at Trusthorpe was proved by events to be sound. New short lengths of curved walls at Huttoft were designed to be stable without support from the backing material and they too suffered little damage. A new wall at Sutton and another opposite the village of Sandilands, both constructed with a wave-return section at the top, were also to give an excellent account of themselves. However, some of these new walls, although structurally sound, were not high enough, and it was above all unfortunate that the poor condition of the neighbouring defences rendered them largely useless.

A new wall had also been constructed at Chapel Point, a very exposed section even on a coast where intense exposure to the elements was the rule rather than the exception. The wall here consisted of a row of steel sheet-piles, 16ft (4·9m) long, tied back to groups of sheet anchor-piles and provided with a stout reinforced-concrete capping beam. A reinforced-concrete flood wall was situated 20ft (6·1m) back from the main piles and the filling was covered with a 6in (0·15m) thickness of reinforced concrete and could not be washed out. There was an additional low-level sheet piled apron round the Point. The foreshore was groyned. It has been calculated that sea-walls on the east coast should be capable of withstanding without fracture distributed pressures of not less than 1 ton per sq ft (10·9 tonnes per sq m) without relying on any support from the backing material. The flood wall here was able to withstand a distributed static pressure per square foot of something less than 4cwt (203·2kg) and hence needed heavier vertical reinforcement.

Further along the coast, north of Ingoldmells Point, was a 1,700ft (518·1m) length of old stepwork which had been patched up a few years previously. One place was in a condition so chaotic that it was known locally as 'Ingoldmells Mess'. This was a particularly dangerous length, because there was no Roman Bank at the rear to contain flooding. Between 1947 and 1948 five new groynes had been built. This wall was in no fit state to withstand a storm surge, although a great point in its favour was the fact that in front of it was an excellent sandy beach gathered and held by the groynes.

South of Skegness the shores of the Wash were for the most part fringed by belts of salt marsh and defended by numerous embankments. In front of the Norfolk Estuary Company's banks extending west and east from the Great Ouse the fairly high-level saltings gave a measure of protection by providing a buffer against the sea.

From Wolferton to Hunstanton was a continuous shingle ridge. For 2 miles (3·2km) from Heacham to Hunstanton a sea-wall had been built on the ridge, divided into three sections. The Heacham South Beach wall was a mass-concrete breast wall 600yd (548·6m) long, with a vertical face. The Heacham North Beach wall, 900yd (822·9m) long, consisted of a reinforced-concrete sloping apron with steel sheet cut-off piling at the toe, and a vertical wall at the top, the whole being supported on concrete piles. Adjoining this was the Hunstanton South Beach wall, 600yd (548·6m) long, having a stepped face with steel sheet cut-off piles in front. At the top of the stepped portion was a promenade 6ft (1·8m) wide, and behind this a parapet wall 3ft (0·9m) high with wave throw-back. Opposite Hunstanton itself was the North Promenade wall. These formed the first-line defences.

The Snettisham Bank, a low earth embankment situated inland from the coastal ridge, and running from the Sandringham

Estate Bank near Wolferton north to Hunstanton, formed the second line of defence. This earth bank had a top level generally only about 2ft (0·6m) above the level of the ordinary high spring tides. During the tidal surge of March 1949 one portion had been breached. Along the tidal Ouse itself the defences consisted of earth banks, whose crest level was generally about 4ft (1·2m) above ordinary high spring tides.

The weaknesses in the defence works in the Great Ouse area were fairly clear. The freeboard provided for the tidal river banks was insufficient to withstand a really high surge. In some places the bank slope was unduly steep and in others the grass cover, either on the slope or at field level immediately behind the bank, was absent or defective. At Magdalen there was a thorn hedge growing near the bottom toe of the bank. Once this was uprooted the speedy erosion of the bank would be inevitable. Along the coast the concrete walls were not strong enough to withstand heavy water pressure and wave impact. Worse, between the northern end of the Hunstanton South Beach wall and the southern end of the North Promenade a gap of 320yd (292·6m) yawned in the defences, effectively rendering the entire defence line useless so far as the safety of Hunstanton itself was concerned. South of the termination of the concrete walls the shingle ridge and the saltings were too low.

It is of course possible to push shingle back by mechanical means to raise its level, and to keep it raised, though this task needs constant attention. Here the situation was not helped by the presence, on or just behind the crest of the ridge, of a motley collection of bungalows and beach huts of the most flimsy construction, which had prevented any remedial work. Another problem was that abnormal and rapid erosion – called 'end erosion' – occurred at the junction of the shingle ridge and the concrete sea-walls, of the kind normally to be expected at the junction of a 'hard' and a 'soft' sea-defence work. Finally the Snettisham Bank had deteriorated to a state where little could be expected of it.

The 116 miles (186·6km) of Norfolk and Suffolk coastline

57

between Hunstanton and Felixstowe were defended by 4 miles (6·4km) of low cliffs, 16 miles (25·7km) of sand dunes, 28 miles (45·0km) of shingle beach and 14 miles (22·5km) of clay bank. In addition there were 252 miles (405·5km) of clay-embanked rivers within this section, ie the Bure, Yare, Waveney, Blyth, Alde, Deben, Orwell and their tributaries. In some places the clay embankments were faced with concrete blockwork. There was an especial need for adequate defences along this difficult section; the coast of Norfolk and Suffolk, bulging into the North Sea, has always been unusually sensitive to storm attack.

The defences between Hunstanton and Blakeney consisted of a series of sand dunes. Further east, in the Cley and Salthouse area as far as Weybourne, the villages and grazing marshes were protected only by a shingle bank. Between Weybourne and Happisburgh the land behind the coast was high; the problem here was one of cliff erosion, in appalling evidence at Overstrand. This small seaside resort had cliffs up to 200ft (60·9m) high, composed of soft sand with small layers of clay and chalk. They were full of springs flowing above the clay layers, which rendered the cliffs unstable and liable to huge collapses, with subsidences of several acres at a time. The beach had a very soft subsoil and had a tendency to severe scouring.

Sea defence here had always been difficult. The remains of two series of collapsed walls on the beach furnished tangible proof of the difficulties. During World War II the neglected defences of the Overstrand Hotel had failed completely, the hotel disappeared over the cliff, and the gap so caused allowed the rest of the defences to be outflanked and progressively undermined. By January 1953 the groynes had disappeared, the beach had rapidly lowered, and the whole of the village was in danger of collapsing into the sea. Because of the obstruction of the ruined walls and the wet, sliding, unstable cliff, the construction of any form of rigid sea-wall had been judged impossible. Hence a timber crib revetment, filled with random concrete and supplemented by steel permeable groynes was commenced, but had not been completed when the storm surge struck the coast.

At Mundesley the sea-wall supporting the promenade was too weak, whilst along 2 miles (3·2km) of coast opposite the three villages of Bacton, Keswick and Walcott a swift and serious spate of erosion had commenced during the autumn of 1952. Here the sea defences had been so inadequate that one tide had engulfed them all. A wall of sorts had been erected – with more haste than discretion – in their place, but it was not only inadequate but was not completed.

At Sea Palling there was no wall at all, merely sand dunes with a highly vulnerable low point where the dunes were crossed by a footpath. This had been used for dragging boats onto the beach, and was heavily trampled, forming a wide, undefended gap. On either side, at Eccles and Horsey, there were concrete walls, rendered largely useless by the situation at Palling. A chain being as strong as its weakest link, little could be expected from the defence line in this locality. Conversely the defences at Caister deserve a special mention, if only because they stood out in startling contrast to the dismal conditions in evidence elsewhere. The village was protected by a well-nigh impregnable sea-wall and was safe against all but the most outrageous attack. The wall had a strong foundation, a sloping revetment and a curved wave-return section at the top.

So far as the esturial works of Norfolk and Suffolk were concerned, these consisted in the main of clay embankments which in general were too low. For example along the Orwell, Stour and Deben estuaries the crest level of the walls in places was as low as $1\frac{1}{2}$ft (0·45m) above, to 6in (0·15m) below, the level of ordinary high spring tides. Where walls of this type had been progressively heightened their tops were vertical, whereas the width of the walls at the base should have been increased. More often than not the back slopes were equipped with a ditch dug hard up to the toe of the wall, which weakened the base of the whole structure. In many estuary areas more remote from the outfalls, the river embankments were almost wholly constructed of peat, not the most satisfactory of materials for use in bank construction. With the advent of pumped drainage of the peat marshes to the rear, and the consequent shrinkage of the land once the water had been abstracted, very serious problems of bank stability had arisen. The shrinkage undermined the foundations, causing the bank to settle and lean inwards towards the marsh. In an attempt to solve the problem long lengths of bank had been fronted with steel and concrete sheet piling. This was no solution as it did nothing to eliminate weaknesses in basic structure.

The clay walls encircling Breydon Water – that huge tidal inlet menacing the rear of Great Yarmouth – were too low, too steep and too weak. The close proximity of a deep ditch to the steep rear face of the walls posed an additional hazard.

Along the Essex coastline there were more than 300 miles (482·8km) of man-made defences barricading its flat marshland borders against inroads of the sea. Included in this figure were the tidal frontages of creeks and estuaries of the rivers Stour, Colne, Blackwater, Crouch, Roach, Thames, Ingrebourne, Roding and Lea. The drained marshlands all lay well below the highest level of spring tides, and were protected from periodic inundation by a clay sea-wall which, along some of the more exposed stretches, was faced with stone slabs. Generally speaking the weaknesses of these defences were identical to those elsewhere along the coast. The walls had a totally inadequate freeboard above the highest tide levels, the concrete blockwork had not been carried high enough up the face of the walls, and the backs needed flattening to an easier slope. Many of the Essex embankments had been raised to barely 3ft (0·9m) above ordinary high spring-tide level.

The situation at Canvey Island, where a settlement of some 11,000 people covering 950 acres had grown up close to sea level, was particularly serious. No adequate defences protected the dwellings although they were vulnerable to flooding on every side, ie from the tidal inlets to the north and west of the town as well as from the Thames itself. The freeboard of the embankments along Benfleet and Holehaven Creeks was almost non-existent in relation to high-tide levels. There was an exceptional risk to many other built-up areas. Along the north bank of the Thames major industrial undertakings including oil refineries, and residential and industrial areas such as East Ham, Barking, Dagenham, Rainham, Purfleet, Grays and Tilbury with their road and rail communications, lay well below maximum tide levels. The defences here consisted mainly of earthen embankments, although there were wharves at a number of industrial sites and occasionally more massive works as, for example, at Tilbury Docks.

In the County of London the defences comprised a variety of structures, such as warehouses, wharves and dock walls, and there were massive walls fronting the Victoria, Chelsea and Albert Embankments. The boroughs of Fulham, Wandsworth, Battersea, Lambeth, Stepney, Poplar, Greenwich and Westminster were very low-lying (see Chapter 7); parts of Bermondsey, the Isle of Dogs and Woolwich were in an even more precarious position. So far as the Thames situation was concerned the authorities had been warned. The consulting engineer Mr C. H. Dobbie, an expert on land drainage and sea defence, writing in the *Journal of the Institution of Civil Engineers* in February 1946, had stated:

> Investigation in the Thames has shown that the wind surge has raised a tide 5ft beyond prediction and that a 7ft surge on such a tide is possible. A joint committee was supposed to set standards for the Thames estuary but this has never been done. It would appear only prudent to increase the usual allowance of 5ft above highest predicted levels.

This standard was never adopted, and in 1953 the authorities had not even begun to carry out the immense works involved.

Further south the Kent defences for the most part took the form of earthen walls with stone facing along exposed sections. Because the subsoil strength of some of the marsh areas was weak, and due to the danger of slips occurring, it had been impossible to carry these to the required height. Also extensive industrial premises caused obstructions. The Erith sea wall adjoining Burt, Boulton & Haywood's timber stores and saw mills was one site where local conditions had prevented the heightening and thickening of the defences by earthwork. Along another section of the walls the proximity of Admiralty oil tanks had limited the width to which the wall could be thickened, and pipes running along the wall had restricted the height to which it could be raised. The Seasalter sea-wall along the Medway estuary was an earthen structure with a light seaward concrete face. Because it ran parallel and adjacent to a public highway no attempt had been made to widen it out at the rear.

The inexorable erosion of the saltings which fronted long sections of the Kent defences increased the potential dangers of the situation. The deepening of the channel of the Thames for navigation had taken its toll. Also during the previous two centuries there had been, particularly in the Medway estuary, large excavations left on the tidal side of the sea-walls where clay has been dug for the manufacture of cement. Further, some expedient should have been devised to counter the effects of attrition against the face of the walls, not only from the tides but also from the increasing volume and size of the river traffic.

None of the Kent tidal defences were really satisfactory. At the Isle of Grain, lying just west of Sheerness, a new oil refinery and some Admiralty installations were insecurely defended by clay embankments which were all too low to contain a tidal surge of any magnitude. At Whitstable not only were several terraces of houses built close to the sea but, being provided with basements, were in a doubly precarious position. The town frontage was very low-lying with a number of shipyards, slipways and boat sheds crowded together along the waterfront, making the problem of sea defence one of almost insoluble complexity. The new sea-wall, completed one month before the 1953 storm, had a totally inadequate freeboard.

But it was from the great Northern Sea Wall, running from Reculver to Birchington, that most trouble could be expected in the event of a break-through of the sea. This wall faced north and had a high degree of exposure, taking the full wave-force when the winds were in a northerly and easterly direction. It was about 3 miles (4·8km) long and linked the Isle of Thanet with the mainland; it also protected about 12,000 acres of marshland and the main highway and railway communications between the Isle of Thanet and the remainder of Kent. It was in process of reconstruction, but the work had not proceeded very far; nevertheless £23,000 had already been spent by the end of January 1953.

This, then, was the condition of the east coast defences between the Humber and Thames estuaries when the 1953 storm struck. All too many areas relied for their sole defence on sagging, archaic embankments with inadequate freeboards, on sea-walls uncompleted although it was mid-winter, on denuded beaches, neglected saltings, eroded sand dunes and attenuated shingle ridges. Disaster was inevitable.

Chapter 5

THE DISASTER

The great east coast flood disaster of 31 January–1 February 1953 exposed in horrific detail the folly of relying on archaic defence structures, of economising unduly on certain aspects of the defence system, even of neglecting it in some localities and, above all, of adopting minimum and not maximum standards of protection. It exposed also the administrative discrepancies – the drawbacks associated with the involvement of local authorities, catchment boards, government departments and private individuals, which had made it possible for anyone to act independently and by so doing upset the balance.

On Saturday, 31 January, flooding started on the Northumberland coast at about 4pm, and during the next nine hours each length of the 1,200 or so miles of sea and tidal defences as far south as the Isle of Thanet was attacked in turn. There was mounting havoc as the surge advanced south. The collapse of the sea-defence system was total and complete; practically the whole length was overtopped or damaged. Breaching occurred at more than 1,000 sites and huge seas swept inland. Thousands of telephones were put out of action and road and rail services were disorganised. Disrupted communications, impassable roads and dislocated essential services engendered the most fearful chaos everywhere, making it difficult for some time to obtain an overall picture of the devastation. The death toll was at first reported as being between 50 and 60. By 9 o'clock on Sunday evening, 1 February, the total had climbed to over 100 'and the figures change every hour'. The final count was 307.

The major part of the disaster occurred in darkness, so there were no eye-witnesses to describe precisely how each wall had failed. Broadly speaking the sea attacked in two ways. In Lincolnshire, north Norfolk and parts of Kent waves hammered against the sea-walls and sand dunes until they were battered and breached; in Suffolk and Essex the sea, surging up the estuaries, overtopped and breached river banks, in a number of cases inundating coastal towns and villages from the rear. In the collapse of the sea defences it was thought that erosion of the face or crest by wave action or scour constituted a dominant factor, whilst there was evidence that the majority of bank failures were preceded by substantial overtopping.

The high sea level and severe wave action generated by the storm winds caused great damage to the natural defences. In some exposed places beaches were scoured away; some were thrown over the sea-walls, the rest swept seawards. Large waves were then able to reach the shore unbroken, where they crashed onto and over the defences, weakening and breaching them. At least a 10yd (9·1m) depth of outer dunes was cut clean away over long stretches of coast. Dunes of no more than 5 to 10ft (1·5–3m) in height were in general demolished; those few which remained were invariably too weak and attenuated to form an adequate defence line. The single belt of dunes near Sea Palling in Norfolk was reduced in width by about 50 per cent. Along lines of cliff the main force of the wave attack was for an hour or more lifted well above beach level and directed at the cliffs themselves. Where these were composed of unre-sistant materials, such as the boulder clays of north Norfolk and the sandy cliffs of Suffolk, the loss by erosion was locally to be measured in yards. All the cliffs along the Norfolk coast yielded a good deal. On the Suffolk coast south of Lowestoft a 40ft (12·2m) high cliff of sand had so much material carried away that the face was driven back 40ft; where the cliff was only 6ft (1·8m) high the face was pushed back 90ft (27·4m). At Kessingland the soft cliff was eaten away behind part of the new sea-wall.

The course of events on 31 January–1 February had considerable significance as it turned out, because it underlined two points: firstly the acute danger of erosion to cliffs well above their bases when the height of the water is at all abnormal, and secondly the incidence of wind and wave. On this occasion the wind blew from the north-west or north-north-west, and places like Heacham, Hunstanton, the entire north Norfolk coast and northern Kent were severely hit. Elsewhere the winds were for the most part offshore and fortunately did not veer round to blow in from the sea. Had they done so – and this point cannot be over-emphasised – the results would have been many times more catastrophic than they were. But the situation was bad enough as it was.

During Saturday afternoon and evening the inhabitants of the east coast went about their customary tasks and occupations, completely unaware of the dire menace advancing on them from the north. Casual remarks might be made about the heavy winds and high tides, but these were normal phenomena on the east coast in January, and thus did not give rise to any general anxiety. For the vast majority of people this Saturday afternoon was no different from any other. At the Harwich and Dovercourt sailing club members were pleasantly occupied in carrying out repairs and renovations to their boats. On Canvey Island many of the residents attended the public ceremony dedicating the new memorial hall to the memory of local men killed in World War II. Saturday evening also saw no interruption in normal activities. The howling winds and lashing seas did not deter people from attending the ambulance competitions being held at the railway club at Parkeston Quay. On Southend pier a dance was in progress, despite the water rising inexorably under the pier structure. People enjoying the show in the Savoy Cinema at Sutton-on-Sea were perfectly oblivious of the fact that disaster was literally lapping at their doorstep; whilst their eyes were glued to the screen water was pouring into High Street through the shattered sea-walls erected to defend the locality against such a storm as this. At Great Yarmouth the usual Saturday night dance was going on at the Floral Hall, whilst floodwater gradually crept up to the steps.

North of the Humber the first defences to suffer serious failure were those of the East Riding of Yorkshire. The sea breached the fatally low cliff and sea-wall just south of Easington, some 4 miles (6·4km) north of Spurn Head. By 9pm the water had advanced more than a mile inland and Easington village square was awash, the sea water flowing in a south-westerly direction, falling into the Humber between Skeffling and Kilnsea. The narrow neck of land affected was an area of strong, fertile soils devoted mainly to arable farming. Simultaneously the flood tide was surging up the Humber, topping and breaching the river banks in a multitude of places. In all, over 4,000 acres of agricultural land in the locality were flooded either directly from the Easington breach or from the Humber. Meanwhile the situation developing along the Humber from East Halton to South Killingholme was giving cause for alarm. Here the clay bank crumbled and the sea smashed through in many places; elsewhere water flowed over, stripping as much as 2ft (0·6m) from the top of the banks. Many homes were progressively swamped. Farmers were able to get most of their stock to high ground but large numbers of poultry were drowned in their pens.

Further to the east, at Grimsby docks, high tide had exceeded that predicted by almost 6ft (1·8m); flooding in this area was extensive and disastrous. Between Killingholme Haven and Grimsby the height of the Humber bank was generally reduced by 3ft (0·9m) and there was a continuous succession of breaches – water thundered through the broken walls inundating houses, factories and farmland. Immingham power station was put out of action, two ships in dry dock there capsized and three factories were thrown out of production for more than a week; the lines of the Immingham light railway were damaged over a distance of some 200yd (182·9m). Several people in the district were rendered homeless. The material damage at Cleethorpes, situated at the mouth of the Humber, was later estimated at around £100,000. The sea poured in torrents

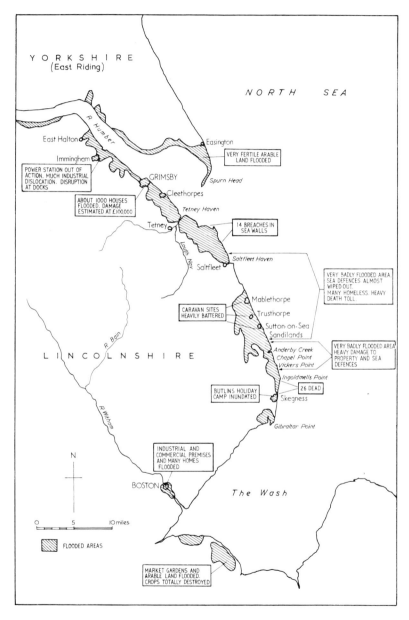

YORKSHIRE
(East Riding)

NORTH   SEA

R Humber

East Halton

Immingham

POWER STATION OUT OF
ACTION. MUCH INDUSTRIAL
DISLOCATION. DISRUPTION
AT DOCKS

ABOUT 1000 HOUSES
FLOODED. DAMAGE
ESTIMATED AT £100,000

GRIMSBY

Cleethorpes

Tetney Haven

Tetney

Loath Nav

Easington

Spurn Head

VERY FERTILE ARABLE
LAND FLOODED

14 BREACHES IN
SEA WALLS

Saltfleet Haven

Saltfleet

VERY BADLY FLOODED AREA.
SEA DEFENCES ALMOST
WIPED OUT.
MANY HOMELESS. HEAVY
DEATH TOLL.

R Bain

L I N C O L N S H I R E

CARAVAN SITES
HEAVILY BATTERED

Mablethorpe

Trusthorpe

Sutton-on-Sea
Sandilands

Anderby Creek
Chapel Point
Vickers Point

VERY BADLY FLOODED AREA
HEAVY DAMAGE TO
PROPERTY AND SEA
DEFENCES

Ingoldmells Point

BUTLINS HOLIDAY
CAMP INUNDATED

26 DEAD

Skegness

R Witham

Gibraltar Point

N

INDUSTRIAL AND
COMMERCIAL PREMISES
AND MANY HOMES
FLOODED

BOSTON

The Wash

O   5   10 miles

FLOODED AREAS

MARKET GARDENS AND
ARABLE LAND FLOODED.
CROPS TOTALLY DESTROYED

Map 2   The Lincolnshire coast, January–February 1953

68

over the concrete apron of the railway embankment and scoured a hole beneath the railway, quickly penetrating to the north end of the town; about 1,000 houses were flooded and choked with sand and silt. On the foreshore wooden buildings were demolished and huge segments of concrete were displaced from the North Promenade. Amusement arcades were awash and the bathing pool at the south end of the promenade was filled with sand and damaged. The main Grimsby–Cleethorpes road was flooded, and the North Cotes RAF Station had to be temporarily evacuated. Much livestock was lost.

But in Lincolnshire it was the exposed central coastal area which sustained the main force of the disaster. Here the sea struck between 5.25 and 7.30pm. Between Donna Nook and Saltfleet Haven there were fourteen breaches in the sea-walls; about 16,000 acres were flooded at Grainthorpe and North Somercotes, wells and bores were contaminated, and telephone and electricity services ceased to function. In this part of Lincolnshire it was the extreme suddenness with which the water rose which constituted so terrifying a part of the ordeal – many families had only minutes to get to places of safety, they had no time to collect possessions. 'There was a roaring sound', said Frederick Drury who had moved to his seaside bungalow at Saltfleet from industrial Rotherham only three months previously. He looked out and 'saw a wave of water coming over the dunes. There was no warning'. Four elderly people were drowned at Saltfleet, and of these perhaps no case was more poignant than that of Mrs Annie Millward. She was eighty and lived alone, but had arranged to ring a bell connected to the house next door if she ever needed help. When the water poured in, her neighbour, now marooned in her own home, heard the bell ringing. The tinkling continued for some time but grew fainter as the water rose. The next day Mrs Millward was amongst those found drowned.

South of Saltfleet floodwater at one time extended in a continuous lake from Mablethorpe to Skegness. The damage

Lincolnshire 1953. Shattered sea-wall at Mablethorpe

sustained by the sea defences along this section of the coast was appalling. At 5.25pm the sea broke through at Sandilands, at the southern end of Sutton-on-Sea. Water swept inland through the breached sandhills. Soon afterwards Sutton-on-Sea High Street was awash, and the water was rising fast. At Mablethorpe the concrete walls were smashed into small pieces and scattered over a wide gap. After the defences opposite the police station had given way at 7.10pm, it was only a matter of minutes before the town centre was flooded to a depth of several feet making it inaccessible from outside. Cars, furniture and household belongings were afloat in the streets, where the gale was lashing the water into huge waves. Nothing could be heard above the roar of the sea and the crashing of flotsam and jetsam but the screams of women and children. Many homes were flooded to a depth of several feet, seagulls were swimming in the fields. Mr George Castleton, who lived in a low-lying part of Mablethorpe, thought it was snowing when he saw something glimmering in his back garden. He opened the door to see, and nearly 4ft (1·2m) of water rushed in, practically knocking him off his feet: 'My wife was sitting by the fire and was swamped. We struggled out to a higher part of the town, but had to leave our dog behind. When we went back . . . he was floating alive on the table.' In addition to the flooding it was estimated that 860,000 tons of sand were washed into the town, leaving the beach a desolate expanse of black clay. In fact the pre-flood level of the beaches between Mablethorpe and Skegness was not fully re-attained in one or two places for several years.

South of Mablethorpe even more serious breaches had been torn in the defences. With each tide, water was ebbing and flowing unchecked through wide gaps, flooding the hinterland to depths of from 1 to 5ft (0·3–1·5m) over an extensive area. At one time the sea penetrated several miles inland behind Sutton-on-Sea, where sand was deposited to depths of from 1 to 8ft (0·3–2·4m) all over the town. Practically every street was impassable. Many houses were completely blocked with sand on the ground floor, whilst debris from the smashed sea-walls and from damaged houses, wrecked furniture and broken fences lay everywhere. There were harrowing stories of tragic ordeals suffered by countless people. Rescuers told of an old man who had had to stand helplessly by and see his crippled wife drown. They told too of a young woman wading in the darkness through the roaring waters, cradling her baby in her arms. She tripped, plunged into the water, and her child was swept away. The death toll in the Mablethorpe–Sutton area was sixteen. The scene here looked like a battle-field. All public services were thrown into chaos or severely impaired. At Acre Gap, between Sutton and Sandilands, the whole of the timber piling defending the locality was washed away, the land was bared to the sea for a distance of 1,400ft (426·7m) and the tide flowed more than 4 miles (6·4km) inland taking the beach with it.

At Sandilands events soon took a turn for the worse after the breach of the sandhills at 5.25pm: the dunes were washed inland, submerging vast acreages of land. Houses were severely damaged or completely destroyed. The concrete step-work, which comprised the main defence line at one point, was not immediately demolished in its entirety, but a few days later began to collapse over its entire length. From Sandilands to Chapel Point the seaward earth bank almost entirely vanished into the sea. It was the second earthen embankment, known as the Roman Bank, which saved the situation. This, comparatively weak though it was and on the point of breaching, managed, albeit by the slenderest of margins, to stem the floodwater, hence saving the district from a huge inundation. Nevertheless Chapel Marsh, situated between the seaward bank and the inner bank, was completely flooded to a depth of 5ft (1·5m) and the devastation was appalling. Many occupied bungalows were sited here; furniture, dead livestock and objects of every description were piled up in a great mound in the lowest part of the marsh. To add to the horrors of the situation the gale was lashing the water into tremendous waves, and hurling some of the debris at the Roman Bank. The entire north side of Anderby Creek was flooded, and the water then banked up, flooding the south side including the pumping station. The force of the water was so great that two buildings, each weighing approximately 15 tons, were moved bodily for a considerable distance. One man was rescued from his flooded home by a boat which sailed into his dining-room, taking him on board halfway up the stairs.

The defences at Chapel Point were heavily battered. Part of the flood-wall broke and overturned; the decking was undermined and badly damaged over a corresponding length; water flowed inland with extreme rapidity. Mr and Mrs T. Walker of Chapel St Leonards commented on the lack of warning. At 6.45 on Saturday evening they were sitting quietly reading in their bungalow, when they were disturbed by the whimpering of their dog Floss. They followed her to the front door, only to find their bungalow surrounded by water. They managed to wade to higher ground, their dog swimming beside them, and spent a wretchedly miserable night, sheltering from the biting wind as best they could in some bushes near their home, returning the next day to collect some clothes and the canary.

A little further south along the coast, from Vickers Point to Butlin's Point near Skegness, the concrete defences were knocked flat and the sea raged in as far as the Roman Bank, resulting in the destruction of property and the loss of six lives at Ingoldmells. The sea also swept into Butlin's holiday camp, which lay under 6ft (1·8m) of water when the sandhills in front of the camp broke. At Skegness about 50 acres of the amusement park and gardens were flooded to depths of up to 5ft (1·5m), a number of buildings and concrete walls were battered, and twenty people perished,

Although the whole flooded area between Mablethorpe and Skegness had been subjected to periodic and severe inundation during past centuries the destruction of life and property in 1953 was probably unprecedented because of the recent crowding of settlements and population into the most dangerous area near the coast, especially into the area seaward of the Roman Bank which was liable to especially deep flooding. Structural damage along this section of the coast was most serious along the sea front, where houses and other substantial buildings and promenades were wholly or partially wrecked, along with the defences upon which they were built. Caravan sites suffered very badly. The severe loss of life can be attributed to the critical depth of the floodwater.

The area bordering the western and southern shores of the Wash was fortunately spared much of the havoc and destruction which the sea wrought north of Skegness, but was not left entirely unscathed. At Boston, on the Witham estuary, where the tide rose more than 6ft (1·8m) above its predicted level, the flooded lower parts of the town lay under water several feet deep. All traffic was brought to a halt to prevent vehicles from driving water with even greater force into the flooded houses. The floodwater spread with devastating speed over a wide area, cascading into houses, churches, warehouses and a cinema. In the Welland and Nene region flooding occurred a considerable distance from the sea due to these rivers overflowing their banks. The banks nearer the sea were actually breached at some places, so that the tidal waters swept unchecked over large acreages of valuable arable land. Fortunately their progress was arrested by the presence further inland of the old Roman Bank which here, as in the central part of the Lincolnshire coast, played a crucial role in mitigating the full effects of the disaster. On the eastern side of the Welland the new sea-bank, protecting hundreds of acres of land, was breached at what, ironically enough, had been considered to be its strongest point. The sea tore a great gap in the defences, bursting through to flood 700 acres of reclaimed marsh which had been drained, levelled and partially reseeded. This land carried some 800 sheep; all but three escaped to higher ground and were ultimately transported to

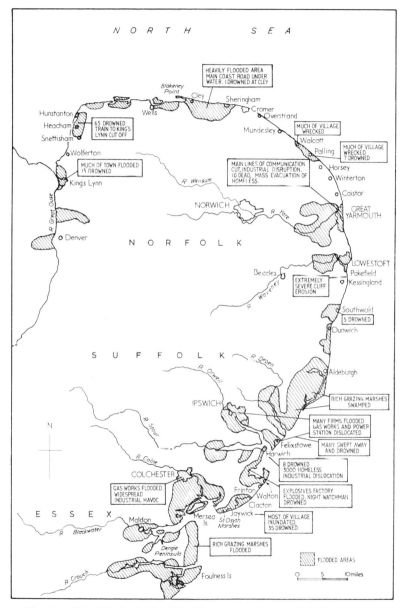

Map 3 The Wash to the Crouch estuary, January–February 1953

Rutland until the crisis was over. Further along the coast the sea-bank was breached, inundating several hundred acres of arable land occupied by smallholders growing such crops as strawberries and bulbs. These, together with considerable acreages of wheat, barley, beans and clover had to be written off as a total loss.

Along the eastern shores of the Wash, which were being heavily battered by on-shore winds, the storm surge dealt a crushing blow to the defences. These were all more or less simultaneously overwhelmed about 7.35pm, at roughly the same time as many places on the Lincolnshire coast were fighting for survival. The crest of the shingle ridge from Wolferton to Hunstanton was cut down and carried anything from 10 to 50yd (9·1–45·7m) inland; because the Snettisham Bank to the rear was much too low, wholesale flooding occurred. There were three major breaches in the shingle ridge, which was cut down to beach level; in the Snettisham Bank there were no less than forty breaches. The Heacham South Beach mass-concrete wall was completely destroyed; the parapet of the Heacham North Beach wall was demolished over a length of 300yd (274·3m) and the face of the wall broken and dislodged; the parapet of the Hunstanton South Beach wall was overturned over a long distance. In the case of both the Hunstanton South Beach and the Heacham North Beach walls the shingle filling at the rear was heavily scoured out.

From Snettisham to Hunstanton all the bungalows and beach huts suffered severe damage after the defences had collapsed. Very many were totally destroyed, whilst others were torn from their positions and carried inland to be deposited at varying distances from the beach, some of them along the King's Lynn–Hunstanton railway line where they posed a considerable hazard. The 7.27pm Hunstanton to King's Lynn train not only collided with a wall of water a short distance from the station, but one of the floating bungalows struck the engine and put it out of action. For six hours the crew of the train struggled to effect temporary repairs and, by using the floorboards of the tender as fuel, managed to raise sufficient steam to crawl back to Hunstanton.

There had been about forty bungalows sited on the low-lying land behind the defences between Heacham and Hunstanton. A number of these buildings, although never intended for permanent occupation, were inhabited and 65 persons were drowned, most of them American servicemen and their families. At the same time an entire street was swept away by the tide which was pouring between the north end of the Hunstanton South Beach wall and the southern end of the North Promenade through the so-called 'Hunstanton Gap'. This had for long constituted a glaring defect along this section of the coastal defences. However, one gleam of light in the prevailing gloom – the more conspicuous by its being an isolated case – was provided by events along the coastline immediately west and east of the river Great Ouse. Here the banks constructed and maintained by the Norfolk Estuary Company successfully withstood the onslaught. A privately owned bank was overtopped and damaged but, since it was not breached, the flooding was limited in extent.

The tidal embankments of the Great Ouse on the whole fared little better than the majority of the coastal defences in the locality. Spilling occurred over the greater part of the 14 miles (22·5km) of river between King's Lynn and Denver sluice. Above Freebridge the west bank was breached in five places. On the east bank there were three breaches of a more serious character which could not be closed immediately because the sites were cut off by water. Of these latter two occurred near the point known as Magdalen Bend. Downstream of Freebridge in the King's Lynn area there were seven breaches. So sudden was the rise of water at King's Lynn itself, and so heavy the spilling over the right bank of the Great Ouse and the left bank of the Nar, that a number of people were trapped in their houses; fifteen were drowned. Soon one-fifth of the town was inundated as water flowed over the river embankments. At West Lynn a series of breaches in the river bank flooded factory premises to a depth of several feet. Land in West Lynn lay under 5ft (1·5m) of water for over two weeks; it was feared it would be uncultivable for five or six years.

To make matters worse there seems to have been considerable alarm unnecessarily generated in the area. Police cars equipped with loud-speakers toured King's Lynn, urging the inhabitants to sandbag their houses against dangers which, as the authorities concerned insisted, were largely mythical. Wild alarmist reports were circulated to the effect that Denver sluice had blown up, exposing the entire southern Fenland to the danger of flooding; that all the tidal banks of the Great Ouse were crumbling and that King's Lynn itself was threatened with total inundation. This unwarranted activity undoubtedly made a decisive and unwelcome contribution to the prevailing confusion. Subsequently the engineer in charge of the Great Ouse defences complained bitterly to his member of parliament.

Meanwhile the storm was striking at the exposed Norfolk and Suffolk coastline. Nothing here, with the exception of the Caister sea-wall, proved capable of withstanding the surge. This strong, well-designed and well-maintained defence withstood the battering of the sea, saved the village behind it, and emerged from the ordeal virtually unscathed. Elsewhere it was a very different story. The adverse reports, each one seemingly worse than the last, flowing into the flood headquarters set up in Norwich during the night of 31 January were received with careful consideration, – perhaps consternation would be the better word. They told of extensive damage to both sea and river defences, the dislocation of all means of transport and collapsed telephone lines. Huge acreages were under water, with particularly large breaches at Wells, Breydon Water behind Great Yarmouth, Aldeburgh and Bawdsey. In east Suffolk there was not a single river estuary or valley which was not affected by the flooding. Between Hunstanton and Wells in Norfolk almost all the land lying between the dunes and the coast road was covered by several feet of water, which had not disappeared by late February. Wells itself sustained heavy damage. Houses in the north-west part of the town were swamped, and the station was under water. A 160 ton vessel was left high and dry on the quay. The Stiffkey valley was flooded, whilst the sea swept over the shingle bank protecting the partially reclaimed Cley and Salthouse marshes, lapped the former sea cliffs behind the coast road, and practically devastated the villages. One person was drowned at Cley. Salthouse looked 'as if it had been hit by high explosives'.

Deep floods penetrated up the Wiveton valley. At Overstrand much of the already precarious walling and parade were badly damaged; the mass-concrete walls were shattered and portions overturned. At Mundesley the sea-wall was undermined at its eastern end, and waves were smashing up the concrete promenade as though it were so much hardboard. The uncompleted sea-wall at Walcott was battered and outflanked; the sea attacked the clay cliffs at the rear, washing away part of the coast road. The main street of Walcott was destroyed and many buildings wrecked. At Palling the waves burst through the trampled gap in the dunes about 8pm, engulfed all the buildings at the seaward end of the village and swept thousands of tons of sand up the village street, to lie there afterwards in drifts 5ft (1·5m) deep. Seven people were drowned. On both sides of Sea Palling, at Eccles and Horsey, the concrete sea-walls were very heavily pounded. The waves overtopped them and cut away the dunes behind. At Eccles the wall collapsed over a length of about 1½ miles (2·5km).

Further along the coast Great Yarmouth was virtually isolated after floodwater had severed all main lines of communication. Here the Cobholm and Southtown areas were badly affected for, besides the overflowing river Yare, they had to contend with floods from behind when the Breydon wall collapsed and tons of water came surging across the marshes, through gaps in the railway embankment and into the streets.

The river started to overflow about 8pm, and people stood

awestruck watching a tremendous wave like the bow-wave of a fast ship curving away on either side of the granite supports of Haven Bridge. A raging flood of water tore towards Southtown and Cobholm. In Ferry Lane bordering the Yare people made futile efforts to erect barricades to protect their homes; the water smashed through, electricity failed, and the streets were plunged into darkness, masking a scene of hideous confusion. A surging mass of evil-smelling floodwater swept along the streets and through houses. Hen coops and rabbit hutches, the animals inside them trapped and drowning, flew past at a tremendous rate, along with boilers, full and empty fish barrels, and debris of every description. Above the din of the roaring water enormous baulks of timber from woodyards bordering the river could be heard crsahing against doors and walls. One smashed through the bedroom window of a house. Then, about 11pm, the Breydon wall gave way. A sheet of water poured ceaselessly through at least three huge breaches, and high walls of spray broke over what was left of the wall. Biting sleet mixed with flurries of snow swept across the marshes. Water from the breaches flowed into Southtown railway station, flooding it to 1ft (0·3m) above the platforms. A signalman was marooned in his box for twenty-one hours before he could be rescued by boat.

Dawn broke on a scene of utter desolation. Cobholm was devastated and much of Southtown. Many people were missing, and hundreds of families were trapped without food or heat in upstairs rooms. Ten people lost their lives, the majority of these elderly women, some living alone, one nearly blind, another lame. Six were drowned; the remaining deaths were attributed to shock. Three of those drowned were swept away by the strong current racing through the street; the remainder perished in their homes. One elderly woman was found by rescuers entangled in an iron bedstead, completely submerged, barely alive. She died soon afterwards.

Yarmouth sea front presented a disastrous spectacle from one end to the other, roads were several feet deep in water, and the police and power stations were flooded. On the marshes adjoining Breydon Water the corpses of cattle were floating about. A reporter surveying the desolate scene saw two pigs, mother and baby, wandering on the railway line desperately seeking shelter from the biting wind, the sole animals alive where hundreds of cattle and pigs were usually grazing.

Across the estuary of the Yare, in Suffolk, events were taking an equally disastrous course. In some places floods covered the land to depths of 7 to 10ft (2·1–3·0m) and ran inland for 3 or 4 miles (4·8–6·4km) or more. Lowestoft was covered with water which came in both behind and over the sea-walls. Five people were drowned at Southwold. Just south of Aldeburgh the sea broke through the shingle bank and through the wall along the river Alde, the water from the two breaches combining to flood the reclaimed land behind the defences with double force. The sea also overwhelmed the grazing marshes of the Deben, Orwell and Stour valleys. Pathetic stories were told by survivors rescued from flooded Felixstowe: 'in the darkness all that could be heard was the roaring of the water and the screaming of terrified women'. The waters rose until they were over the top of rows of prefabricated houses, and twenty-eight people clinging to the roofs were washed away and drowned.

Further south, across the river Stour, the tidal defences of Essex fronted the open sea and wound round creek and estuary. The two distinct parts of the Essex coastline reacted in different ways to the surge. Along the cliff coast to the north the abnormal rise of sea level allowed the waves to break higher up the beach and undercut the base of the clay cliffs. Huge falls resulted. Along the embanked coast of south Essex the defences were overwhelmed with the same devastating speed as those of Lincolnshire, Norfolk and Suffolk.

By 1am on 1 February the sea-walls had begun to collapse as far up the Thames estuary as Tilbury. The sea broke through in one place after another in rapid succession. Of the

308 miles (496km) of tidal defences maintained by the Essex River Board, 155 were breached, overtopped, weakened or otherwise damaged. In the 67 miles (108km) of wall which failed outright there were hundreds of breaches, some up to 50yd (45·7m) wide and from 5 to 20ft (1·5–6·1m) deep. Frontages not maintained by the river board encountered a similar fate. Of the 25 miles (40km) belonging to the War Department more than two were breached down to ground level, apart from less serious damage on other lengths. Harbour, dock and wharf frontages, for example at Walton, Clacton, Maldon and Southend, were overtopped and damaged. In a 5 mile (8km) stretch from Foulness Point towards Shoeburyness, one-third of the entire length of sea-wall disappeared.

On Canvey Island forty breaches, in width varying from 10 to 200ft (3·0–60·9m) were made in the defences. The northern part of the island suffered most; the embankment adjoining the South Benfleet creek gave way in many places as floodwater surged up the narrowing channel. In the same area the recently completed Coryton oil refinery was flooded after a break in the sea-wall. The situation was made infinitely worse by the fact that when the ebb came it was inconsiderable. Thus, where the walls were overtopped they were in places overtopped for a long time; where they were breached water poured through over a lengthy period, scouring the breaches wider and deeper, not only on the flow but on the ebb also.

More than 49,000 acres in Essex were flooded. Of these 41,760 were agricultural land; the rest were built-up areas, carrying a high concentration of people, buildings and industrial plant. The greater part of the coastal fringe was flooded on average $\frac{1}{2}$ mile (0·8km) inland. Sodden farmland was everywhere in evidence. There were 113 deaths and 13,088 people were driven from their homes. Thousands had to be evacuated from Canvey Island, whilst hundreds were moved from the Tilbury and Purfleet areas. Some of the biggest losses were sustained in the south of the county, where the disaster struck with hideous force. All the islands on the north bank of the Thames estuary were completely swamped – a month later they were still under water.

The surge first struck Harwich, built on a small peninsula jutting out into the Stour estuary in the extreme north of the county. By 10.13pm the tide was flowing over the quay. Here there soon developed a scene of unbelievable chaos. The town was simultaneously attacked from three sides and by midnight water was pouring in from east, north and west. The quay, the esplanade and the Bathside area to the west were all flooded and the pier submerged. The water in Bathside piled up between the Stour road and the railway embankment, surging up one street and down another, pouring in torrents into basement areas and into yards and gardens below street level. An eye-witness gave a graphic account of the water 'rolling up the street in waves – almost like the Severn Bore – and with it garden fences, gates and debris of all kinds'. The whole of Harwich from the quay to the police station lay huddled in several feet of water. Three thousand people were homeless. Great lumps were washed out of the railway embankment, Harwich Town station was flooded, the continental pier damaged and the train-ferry berthing gear put out of action. Eight people were drowned, including a young mother and baby and a man who lost his life trying to save them. Two of the other flood victims were bedridden, one of these drugged with sleeping tablets. At the Anchor public house the landlord and his wife had gone down to the cellar to try to remove some of the smaller barrels of beer to safety. Simultaneously water burst in from the street and garden through three doors at once. The landlord's wife managed to escape, but the rush of water slammed the cellar door behind her, sweeping her up to the top of the stairs. Her husband was trapped in 15ft (4·5m) of water below. Rescuers ultimately had to cut through the floor of the bar to reach his body.

At Parkeston Quay, Harwich, the railway embankment was breached at both ends; station, locomotive depot and goods yard were inundated. Between Parkeston and Dovercourt, immediately south of Harwich, $\frac{1}{2}$ mile (0·8km) of track was washed away. Southwards along the coast beach huts at Walton and Frinton were ripped from their sites and floated out to sea. Between 10pm and midnight flooding began to develop inland also, as the swollen tide advanced inexorably up the estuaries of the Stour, Colne, Blackwater and Crouch, leaving a trail of devastation in its wake. By 10.30pm the water in Maldon, at the head of the Blackwater estuary, was spilling over the promenade into the bathing pool. This had a capacity of $2\frac{1}{2}$ million gallons (11·2 million litres) and was empty; within twelve minutes it was full. Acres of agricultural land, both pasture and arable, were engulfed, barns and houses flooded, and boats torn from their moorings. Farmhouses and outbuildings sited on rising ground in the marshland bordering the Dengie peninsula, between the rivers Blackwater and Crouch, were gradually encircled by water. Their occupants awoke next morning to find themselves cut off, the floods actually lapping their doorsteps.

Meanwhile the situation at places like Walton and Jaywick was being complicated by the presence nearby of backwaters, tidal inlets and estuaries, exposing the towns not simply to a frontal attack but, as at Great Yarmouth and Harwich, to attack from many sides. Jaywick in particular was in a state of complete disorganisation, swamped by 2,000 million gallons (9,000 million litres) of water which in some places lay 6ft (1·8m) deep. By 1.45am on Sunday morning there were twenty-two breaches in the sea-wall fronting the north bank of the Colne estuary, from which a torrent of water headed east across the St Osyth marshes. The lie of the ground channelled it inexorably towards the back of Jaywick where no danger had been anticipated. As the torrent advanced its speed was increased by the driving wind and its volume reinforced by water flowing in from thirty breaches along the St Osyth beach. Such was the force and impetus of the current that it stripped the grass off the marshland as it passed over it. Most of the caravans on the marsh were smashed to pieces and the floodwater, in its headlong progress towards Jaywick, bore debris from the wreckage along with it. When the water reached Jaywick it rose so fast in some places that people were drowned in their beds. The village was entirely inundated apart from one small island of dry ground, and the survivors were stranded on roof-tops, windowsills, even on the top of wardrobes, tables and draining-boards, where they had clambered to safety. Thirty-five people were drowned. Two more bodies were recovered from the flooded stores at nearby Point Clear Bay.

In the meantime events on Foulness Island had taken equally as critical a turn as those at Jaywick. By 2am the only road connecting Foulness to the mainland was under water. Access by boat was all but impossible due to high winds and heavy seas. At dawn on Sunday morning Foulness was seen to be virtually one expanse of water as far as the eye could see, with here and there the tops of gates and fences, a few trees and the occasional haystack visible. People were stranded in upstairs rooms, whilst the animals were, if possible, in an even worse plight. An eyewitness account described how they were 'travelling about the fields, swimming from one place to another. Several were drowned in the deep water – particularly sheep. Others became entangled in fences. Poultry houses were tipped over or floating about. Partridges and pheasants took refuge in trees and on stacks; rabbits were observed floating on pieces of timber, and even up trees.' The floods claimed other victims. Three people were drowned.

Nearby Wallasea Island was also completely submerged, and here there were two fatal casualties. The body of an auxiliary postman was not recovered until 8 March, when it was found in a ditch behind the sea-wall. One of the guests at the Creeksea Ferry Inn was trapped and drowned when water swept into the building.

Simultaneously the floods hit Great Wakering a little further to the south. Here there was a temporary housing estate of

85

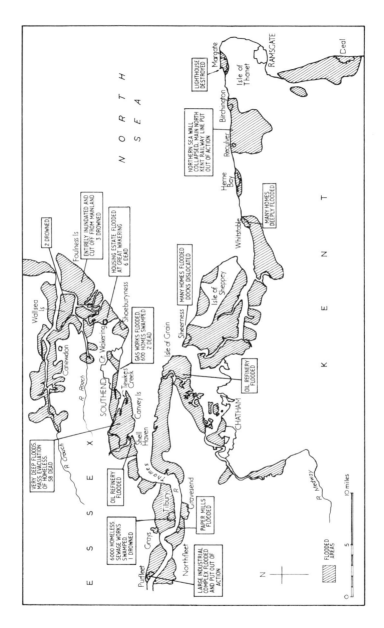

Map 4 The Thames estuary, January–February 1953

thirty-four Nissen huts sited in a hollow in the middle of the common. Water began flowing into the estate about 1am on Sunday morning through an enormous breach in the sea-wall at Morrins Point. The occupants were awakened by a trickling sound. Many thought they had forgotten to turn the taps off, and got out of bed to find the sea forcing its way under their doors. Dazed as they were by this calamity some few made a bid to escape, and waded out of the estate carrying the children, at first knee deep and then up to the waist in water. But as the flood grew deeper and flowed with a stronger current those remaining were afraid to venture out. Instead they clambered through the windows on to the corrugated roofs, clinging precariously, most of them dressed in nothing but their night clothes, battered by gusts of wind and in imminent danger of being hurled down into the icy flood-waters swirling menacingly below. One elderly couple, unable to reach the roof, climbed on to their stove, where they stood for nine hours up to their chests in water. Eventually four bodies were recovered from the Nissen huts – those of an elderly couple and of a young mother and child. All had been drowned. Two others, a child and an elderly man, later died in hospital from shock and exposure.

Meanwhile the scene at neighbouring Southend had assumed a vastly different aspect from the 'Sunny Southend' of the holiday posters. Between 12.15 and 12.30am the sea front had been flooded over its entire length, and the Southend works of the North Thames Gas Board inundated. Six hundred homes were flooded, and acres of glasshouses smashed, their crops ruined. The situation was complicated by outbreaks of fire, probably the result of electrical 'shorting'. There were two deaths: an elderly man stepped out of bed into sea water and died of shock; another elderly man died of pneumonia, which had been aggravated by his prolonged immersion in icy water.

But the destruction wrought by the surge along the east coast nowhere took a more tragic turn than on Canvey Island, a little to the west of Southend. The disaster here gave a stern warning of the risks involved in the development of settlements of any size close to sea level without adequate protection. It was Canvey Island which rivetted the nation's attention as the full horror of what happened during the early hours of 1 February became known. By midnight the sea was flowing over the low and decrepid Tewkes Creek embankment 'like a waterfall'.

Between 12.30 and 2.00am the Canvey inhabitants were literally fighting for their lives, face to face with the stark imminence of death. Some few had been warned, just in time, to take refuge in their attics and lofts; in the Sunken Marsh area, adjoining Tewkes Creek, most of the inhabitants had no warning at all. They were awakened at about 1.10am by a roar as the nearby sea-wall was breached and the water thundered past their doors in an irresistible avalanche. Within fifteen minutes the water was above windowsill level, sweeping towards the High Street, joining up with other areas already flooded, and spreading in every direction. A resident of the Newlands estate in the Sunken Marsh recorded his profound sense of shock 'as the door flew open and icy water poured in'. Somehow, dazed with sleep and numb with horror, he struggled upstairs. The water rose steadily: 'it was a surging torrent, all manner of things carried by it, including a caravan, several sheds, and any amount of heavy timber, and several water tanks'. These were tossed hither and thither by wind and water, adding their weight to the fearful din by knocking against the walls and doors 'like battering rams'. Many people were drowned in bed. Others died of shock or exposure as they scrambled on to house roofs and waited in the dark and paralysing cold for help to come. One man drowned clinging to the branches of a tree he had climbed in an effort to escape the rising floodwaters.

Others were more fortunate. Mr Charles Stevens and his wife Elsie both had a miraculous escape. Mr Stevens described how they were 'in bed . . . the dog woke me with its barking. I got up to see what the matter was and found my feet in water. Minutes later the whole bungalow was flooded. If it hadn't been for the dog we would have drowned as we slept'. Mr Stevens scrambled on top of a wardrobe and punched a hole in the plaster ceiling of the building, dragging his wife and children through onto the roof: 'Then we waited eleven hours to be rescued.' Beneath them the bungalow was almost completely full of water: 'It was cold and dark and we were soaking wet. All around us people were screaming for help.' Across the road lived the Stevens's daughter and son-in-law. They were trapped in their home, but spent the last few terror-ridden minutes of what remained to them of life in trying to float their baby Linda to safety, using her pram as a boat. One of the rescue workers eventually pulled her out alive. Her parents, whose last thoughts had been only of her, were drowned.

Shortly after the catastrophe a Canadian correspondent found Canvey:

> a town in the sea . . . a grey, grim, sad place. Sad because, as I saw, the dead found in the broken dykes still come slowly down the streets in rowboats. And specially sad because at times there are still women trying to push back past the police and the soldiers, to go wading themselves in search of their own missing or dead. The searchers fear and know that they'll find more bodies in the broken dykes of Newlands Marsh, and it's from Newlands Marsh that the rowboats come slowly in along the street, sometimes with a sad burden wrapped in blankets.

A fireman, Micky Sanders, later described how the 'worst thing was finding the bodies of people you had known all your life. We had to lay about 18 or 20 bodies out on the pavement to be identified. They were all people I actually knew. You can't imagine what it was like'.

The death toll on Canvey Island was fifty-eight. Whilst many of the victims were drowned in their beds by the torrents of water which burst without warning into their homes, others were trapped in deep water for hours. Their's was a particularly agonising end. Clinging to floating furniture, hanging on to doors, standing on sinks or stoves, sometimes up to the chin in icy water, or crouching on rooftops, many collapsed and slipped from places of comparative safety into the water. Others simply died of shock and exposure. On Canvey, as elsewhere, the official death roll made no allowance for those whose lives were cut short by the nightmare conditions which they endured that night. Especially vulnerable were the old, the young, those living alone, and those prone to respiratory or rheumatic illnesses. On Canvey at least it was noted that the death rate climbed significantly during the two months following the disaster, as compared with the same two months the previous year. But despite death and disaster the indomitable spirit of the islanders shone through at every stage of the catastrophe, and was typified by the erection of a signpost, the message it bore defiant of wind and tide: 'Bear up. Canvey will live again.'

At the same time that Canvey Island was facing disaster a hammer blow was being struck at Tilbury, further westwards along the Thames estuary. Between 12.40 and 1.15am some streets were flooded more than waist deep. One boy discovered his dog floating around on a large cake tray. Hardly a house escaped damage in some form; more than 6,000 people were homeless. Plant at the sewage works was submerged, creating additional problems. An old lady, seventy-nine years old, living alone, was trapped by floodwater in a downstairs lavatory and drowned. Simultaneously disaster struck the Canning Town area of West Ham. The inflow of nearly 142 million gallons (640 million litres) of water effectively converted a densely built-up area of about 250 acres of factories, shops, railways, commercial undertakings, schools, churches and over 1,100 houses into a lake. In the flooded premises of William Ritchie & Son the night-watchman escaped drowning by fleeing up to the first floor, only to be

Damage to the Kent defences, January 1953: The old sea-wall at Nagden breached by the flood

killed by coal gas escaping from a fractured main.

Even central London caught the tail-end of the catastrophe. Water actually lapped the top of the parapet along the Victoria and Chelsea embankments and Millbank. The defences were overtopped by a few inches between Greenwich Pier and London Bridge, and by about 1in (2·5cm) just upstream of Woolwich. At the same time the southern shore of the Thames estuary and the north Kent coast were being heavily battered.

The coast of north Kent, with its marshes and intervening stretches of clay cliff, is in many respects similar to that of Essex on the opposite side of the Thames estuary. But one difference is of paramount importance in assessing the effects of the surge in the two areas. Whereas the Essex coast is relatively sheltered from north and north-westerly gales, the Kent coast is fully exposed to their fury. In 1953 almost the whole length of the Kent River Board's coastline was over-topped, from Woolwich in the west as far eastward as Birchington. The damage to the sea defences was catastrophic, with about 400 major or minor breaches, frequently some hundreds

91

of yards in length. More than 50,000 acres of land were inundated and in several urban districts seawater lay 9ft (2·7m) deep. This unprecedented flooding underlined with particular force the fact that the defences here, as almost everywhere else along the east coast, were both too low and too weak to withstand the onslaught.

The first intimation of disaster received by the Kent River Board was a telephone call to the deputy engineer, shortly after midnight on Sunday morning, from an official of the Anglo-Iranian Oil Company whose refinery was situated at Grain, at the junction of the Thames and Medway estuaries. He explained how water was pouring over the top of the sea-walls into the refinery. Worse news followed: that flooding was taking place in the low-lying areas and that, in the course of a few minutes, breaches had occurred over almost the whole length of the sea-walls from Woolwich to Birchington. At Dartford there were several gaps in the river bank, and water was surging through the flood barriers. The power station was inundated and the night shift cut off. In the town centre, shop windows were blasted out by two explosions

Damage to the Kent defences, January 1953: The Northern Sea Wall: main breach west of Brooksend

caused by water pouring into Joseph Wells's fireworks factory at Long Reach. At the New Northfleet paper mills, staff rowed round the building in boats. Mrs Lucy Randall, the canteen manageress, found rashers of bacon and bits of macaroni floating in the water: 'All gas and electricity was off so we cooked sausage and mash and soup on a primus stove. It was a very small stove and we were trying to feed 200 mill workers and firemen from it.' In the Gordon Gardens at Gravesend the statue of the famous Victorian general stood waist-high in sea water.

At Sheerness on the Isle of Sheppey a tidal wave swept over the Cheyney Rock defences and poured into homes in the lower part of the town. There were incredible scenes at the docks, where the submarine *Sirdar* was in dry dock. Suddenly the sea came rushing in filling it to a depth of 36ft (11m). The helpless submarine sank and alongside it the frigate HMS *Berkeley Castle* capsized. An eye-witness described the chaotic scene: 'The damage was phenomenal. The *Berkeley Castle* had her bow lifted up onto the dock wall with her stern at the bottom of the water. The submarine had to go for scrap.' The Isle of Sheppey was cut off, the bridge over the river Swale being marooned in the middle of an expanse of water 4 miles (6·47km) wide. Half the island was submerged and three-quarters of the town of Sheerness.

Sea water poured into basement houses at Whitstable over the new sea-wall. Rescue workers found an elderly couple standing on the kitchen sink, and even then half under water. Several timber shacks were partially destroyed, a large quantity of shingle was washed over the wall into the gardens of houses near the front, and a number of boats were driven into basement rooms. Hundreds of oyster barrels were washed out of the Whitstable Oyster Fishery Company's store, and drifted about the streets. Herne Bay fared no better. At first light on Sunday morning the resort presented a scene of incredible devastation. Huge lengths of the promenade were covered by thousands of tons of shingle. At the pier head the road was blocked by a 4ft (1·2m) wall of smashed rowing boats, shattered concrete posts and sand. Hundreds of deeds and documents were ruined when water swept into the strong rooms of the urban council offices. Many houses and shops facing the sea were flooded. A resident of Beach Street described how:

> At half-past one our back wall was broken down and the sea rushed in the downstairs windows. We thought it was all up for us. We retreated upstairs and watched the level of the water rising by the light of the gas jet burning in the hall. We were trapped until a policeman came down the street in a boat banging at the windows, and then we climbed down a ladder and were rowed to dry land.

The residents of Beltinge, ten miles east of Whitstable, were aghast at the spectacle of a cliff which had advanced over 100yd (91·4m) inland to the edge of their once-secluded lawns. For a distance of nearly 1 mile (1·6km) the cliff – undermined by the persistent pounding of heavy seas – had subsided to produce a landscape described by onlookers as 'like the face of the moon'. The cliff-top road, gates and big sections of land belonging to the Miramar Hotel had dropped straight down, and were 'laid out in a crazy pattern at the bottom . . . together with the drains and fences, still standing upright'. But there were even worse disasters. The little town of Seasalter, to the west of Whitstable, was destroyed. There were breaches in the Northern Sea-Wall between Reculver and Birchington hundreds of yards long. At Birchington a section of wall backed by a natural low chalk cliff was eroded back to the solid chalk. An adjacent stretch of unbacked wall was obliterated. The main London–Margate railway line was flooded between Reculver and Birchington, and considerable lengths of rail were swept off the embankment.

Margate itself was heavily pounded. Great gaps were torn in the concrete facing of the promenade. The 60ft (18·3m) high lighthouse at the end of the jetty at the entrance to

Margate harbour was undermined and fell into the sea. Walls of water swept into the Classic cinema where – ironically – the current film was entitled *Whirlpool*. The narrow streets leading to the harbour were choked with refuse and broken boats, and the police station was flooded. At the height of the storm Margate was blacked out, but at Dreamland, which switched on its own plant, the Saturday night dance continued in the ballroom, although the music of the band was sometimes drowned by the shrieking of the wind and the roar of the waves battering the promenade outside.

Miraculously only one person in Kent – a sluice-keeper on the Belvedere marshes – died; it was the livestock which suffered a heavy death toll. The road connecting the Sportsman inn at Seasalter with the Thanet Way was blocked with the bodies of drowned sheep. On the coastal marshes cattle stood huddled together on little hummocks surrounded by water, some already dead, some dying, the rest enduring the appalling conditions with the dumb fortitude of their kind. Many were rescued despite the daunting obstacles. Two men, a farmer and a fireman, floating on a makeshift raft of four telegraph poles lashed together, paddled out in 14ft (4·2m) of freezing water to rescue forty cows stranded on an island of dry land. They were successful, and the animals swam to safety.

As in Kent, agriculture and industry along the entire coast, from Humber to Thames, were very badly hit. Most waterside business premises along the east coast – shipyards, timber yards, maltings, mills and granaries – suffered in some form or another, whether by outright damage, suspended production or dislocated communications. Transport sustained acute local disruption. Two hundred and twenty miles (354km) of track and eighty stations were temporarily out of service. Premises of London Transport, British Road Services and the Tilling Group were flooded. The Humber ports and the docks at King's Lynn suffered, as also did stocks in the warehouses. Factories were under water along the Humber, at King's Lynn, Yarmouth and Harwich. The isolated 160 acre site of the Great Oakley works of the Explosives & Chemical Products Company on Bramble Island in Essex was completely inundated, in some places to a depth of 10ft (3m). The nightwatchman stumbled about, waist-high in water, and was drowned. His body was washed ashore at Felixstowe many weeks later. Apart from individual concerns scattered round the coast, the firms which suffered most damage were those clustered in the business areas round the Yare, the Orwell estuary and at Colchester Hythe at the head of the Colne waterway, but above all in the dense industrial concentrations along the Thames.

At Great Yarmouth factories and workshops were flooded and machinery rendered unusable. Records were lost and goods washed into the river and out to sea. Many firms were under water for lengthy periods. At the engineering works of Pertwee & Back Ltd the river water, mingled with oil and mud, swept through the garage, the foundry and the workrooms. Moulds – the work of many weeks – in the foundry were completely destroyed. Everything was caked with mud and filth. Oil drums from Batley's Garage in Southtown floated up and down the streets and through houses. At Clarke's Mill thousands of sacks of wheat were affected by floodwater. At the warehouses and mill of J. & H. Bunn Ltd it proved impossible to estimate the damage to grain, feeding stuffs and fertilisers.

In the Orwell estuary twenty-two firms, a gasworks and a power station were completely dislocated. At Colchester Hythe the factory of Crosse & Blackwell Ltd was flooded, with extensive damage to foodstuffs. The printing works of Spottiswoode, Ballantyne & Co Ltd was put out of action. Water poured into the timber yards of Brown & Sons Ltd and Groom Daniels. The Colchester Lathe Company – situated so far back from the river that it had never occurred to anyone that its premises would ever be threatened – was inundated and all the machinery submerged. Water burst into the brickworks of Moler Products Ltd from the rear, flooding the power house and rectifiers. On the west side of the Hythe the flow bulldozed its way into the gasworks putting out the boiler fires. But it was the extensive undertakings along the Thames that sustained the worst injury. The earthen sea-wall adjoining Callender's Cable Works was badly overtopped and the works put out of action for several weeks. During the early hours of Sunday morning water poured through breaches in the seawalls at both Shell Haven and Coryton. The whole of the Vacuum Oil Company's new refinery was flooded; plant worth £30 million was standing idly in the water, production of petrol having ground to an abrupt halt. Meanwhile water spreading from the Vacuum Oil Company's site was flowing into the Shell Haven Refinery, a huge complex and one of England's leading production centres of petroleum fuels for transport and industry. The flooding here was extensive, affecting the labour office, accounts department, office services, the garage, loading-bays, canteen and medical centre, whilst closing down the central boiler house together with the steam air compressor. Production was disrupted for several days.

Flood damage to industry: The Shell–BP site at Purfleet. The white objects are partly submerged rolls of paper from a nearby mill

But this was nothing compared to what was happening further west, at Purfleet, where there occurred an industrial catastrophe of the first magnitude. Failure of the wall in front of the Purfleet Deep Wharf & Storage Company's site had allowed the Thames to pour down into the marshland plain occupied by several factories and industrial premises. Here the water lay more than 10ft (3·0m) deep in some places, obliterating the Fenchurch Street to Tilbury railway line and swamping all the plant, buildings, installations and transport of the businesses concerned. The Purfleet Deep Wharf & Storage Company's site, occupying more than 40 acres, presented at daybreak on Sunday a hideous spectacle. It lay under several feet of water which was washing round the tarpaulined stacks of over 65,000 tons of raw sugar. Stored on the site were more than 50,000 reels of newsprint, thousands of which were afloat and drifting in all directions, some into adjacent works, others across the marshes over an area of several miles. Some eventually came to rest in a sluice where they so effectively clogged the workings that it was unable to evacuate any of the 30 million tons of floodwater that had flowed into the area. Next door at the Esso Petroleum site nine large storage tanks were ripped from their foundations and the pipelines dislocated.

At the Shell-Mex & BP site the confusion defied description. Tanks floated away and electric pumps were submerged. About 1,000 oil barrels, many of them full, were scattered far and wide, and stacks of metal oil containers were thrown down. Pump houses, fitters' shop and boiler house were all under water. Buildings were damaged and records lost. Water also broke into the Thames Board Mills, where conditions in the works were described as 'a scene of fantastic desolation and chaos'. At the nearby margarine factory of Van den Berghs & Jurgens the water in some places was up to the ceilings, and equipment sustained irreparable damage. Conditions throughout the entire industrial complex were of the most dismal. Debris in the form of swollen reels of newsprint each weighing more than half a ton, bales of waste paper, bags of sugar, oil

Flood damage to agriculture: A typical view of flooded farmland along the east coast

drums and barrels drifted, bumped and jostled hither and thither. Thousands of sugar bags had burst into the water which was already slimy with oil. Altogether hundreds of thousands of pounds-worth of damage had been done.

Agriculture too was badly hit by the floods. Livestock losses were severe, although amongst the large animals the casualty figures were astonishingly low considering the circumstances, due to the natural instinct of loose animals to bolt for higher ground. A large percentage of the cattle drowned were either tied up or in cattle yards. Apart from this many cows became chilled through standing about in the damp and had to be sold for slaughter. One Essex bull stood for thirty-six hours up to his neck in water, but survived. Inevitably many animals were left to fend for themselves. In Lincolnshire some sheep managed to climb onto the sand hills. One pig showed infinite resource by taking shelter on top of a potato clamp, eating the potatoes and making its bed in the warm straw down to which it had rooted through the outer covering of soil. In Essex thirteen pedigree Friesian heifers found refuge on the mound of a duck decoy, and in Kent livestock stood about on knolls and on the sea-walls – what remained of them – pathetic huddled groups, marooned in a huge expanse of water.

Farm buildings suffered to a varying degree; temporary structures, such as lean-to sheds and poultry houses, invariably sustained serious damage. Feeding stuffs were ruined in barns, and outside a considerable quantity of coarse fodder was washed away. Stocks of fertilisers were destroyed, and a large quantity of agricultural machinery submerged, much of it damaged beyond recovery. Huge areas of pasture and arable land were flooded, and even the famous Kent orchards did not escape the disaster; about 600 acres of some of the finest apple, pear and cherry trees were written off as a total loss. Every kind of farm enterprise suffered, including market gardens and smallholdings. Along some sections of the coast glasshouses were flooded and wrecked, and considerable acreages of market-garden land inundated.

After the floodwaters had receded the coastal grazing marshes without exception presented a sorry spectacle, with acres of dying grass. To many observers it seemed a pleasant sight to see the sun's rays, slanting across the marshes, cause myriads of salt crystals on the grass to glisten and sparkle; this was sinister evidence, however, of the great quantities of salt to be absorbed by the ground or washed away by rain. In addition there was a large acreage of land which, although never actually submerged, became thoroughly saturated by salt water backing up the drains, ditches and under-drains into the soil of the fields. The effects of this could be expected to show up in the crops later on. In some localities the internal drainage system itself was acutely disrupted, both from the channels being choked with silt and from the after-effects which gave rise to severe slipping on the sides of drains.

But great as had been the devastation along the east coast of England, the floods in the south-west Netherlands – where the low-lying land reclaimed from the sea was almost entirely protected by dykes and dunes – were even worse. This was almost undoubtedly the result of direct on-shore winds working over an abnormally high sea level. Along the English coast the winds had been for the most part off-shore and sea-levels not quite so high. The area worst affected was concentrated between Rotterdam and the Scheldt, and included the greater part of the islands forming the province of Zeeland which comprised land wrested from the sea over the past 700 years. The most sorely stricken were the island of Schouwen-Duiveland, nine-tenths submerged, and the neighbouring island of Overflakkee, which was reduced to a bleak grey lagoon surrounded by earth embankments. Apart from agricultural land some towns were wholly or partly inundated. More than fifty dykes burst simultaneously and nearly half a million acres of polder country were swallowed by the sea. Heavy casualties occurred. Some 1,800 people died and about 100,000 had to be evacuated. The toll of livestock, houses and farms was colossal, total damage being estimated at about £100 million. From the economic standpoint, especially as regards agriculture, the consequences of the disaster presented a major national problem. Had the floods reached the industrial areas in any volume, damage to the national economy might well have proved fatal.

Chapter 6

AFTERMATH OF DISASTER

On the morning following the disaster, and for some days to come, newspaper headlines spelt out the hideous news to a shocked nation: 'Tidal Wave Horror' – 'Worst Floods in Memory' – 'Thousands Homeless' – 'Animals Drowned on Marshes'. The 'Lincolnshire havoc' was 'worse than Lynmouth', whilst 'The angry sea pours into Kent like straining veg. in a colander.' By the way events along the east coast had developed during the surge, it was apparent that the widespread devastation would be far beyond the scope of ordinary first-aid measures. 'It is already clear', commented the Minister of Agriculture in the House of Commons on Monday, 2 February 1953, 'that this disaster confronts us with the need for reinstatement of sea defences along a great length of our coastline.' In point of fact the entire system was sufficiently defective to require a massive overhaul. The Home Secretary, in his broadcast to the nation on the same day, stressed that the storm surge represented a national disaster:

> To the nation's grief there has been a severe loss of life and hundreds of persons are still missing. We do not yet know the full scale, but as the Prime Minister has stated, the catastrophe must be treated upon a national basis and as a national responsibility. In particular, he assured Parliament that financial support for personal relief and for emergency repairs will be available. In a disaster such as this, sympathy can best be shown by affording unstinted help and work, and the Government feel sure that the nation will, as is its wont, rise to the emergency.

The Government did not ask in vain. The heartfelt words of gratitude later expressed by one of the Canvey Island flood victims summed up the situation:

> Everywhere helping hands were there to care for and comfort us and now we are picking up the threads again with a nice feeling inside that our people have got a wonderful store of warm fellowship which is not always apparent, but it's there.

The stricken areas were inundated with gifts of every description. They poured in, not only from every corner of the British Isles, but from all over the world. Food, sweets, toys, furniture, bedding, crockery, fuel and money were given by manufacturers, local tradesmen and private individuals. In addition offers of accommodation for the homeless, from prospective foster-parents for orphans, offers of sandbags and sandbaggers, of drivers and transport, plant and machinery of every description, offers to do anything that was wanted, were received in an endless stream of sympathy and goodwill. The first essentials were to house and feed the homeless and destitute, and to trace those who, in the indescribable chaos that had broken loose in the disaster areas, were still missing. Rest centres, feeding centres, mobile canteens and clothing distribution centres had been organised with amazing rapidity, and rescue operations by police, firemen and the ambulance service were going on unremittingly under the most daunting conditions.

The problems seemed endless, for apart from the toll it had taken in human lives and suffering, there was the heavy damage that the storm had inflicted on agricultural land and on industry. Flooding of any kind waterlogs the soil and excludes air from it, but land flooded by salt water causes extra difficulties in that the effect of the deposited residues of salt is more serious and persistent. Common crops will not grow if there is a high concentration of salt in the soil. Some can tolerate more than others. Sugar beet will stand 2 tons of

103

salt per acre of soil, barley perhaps $2\frac{1}{2}$ tons and common grasses from 3 to 5 tons. In 1953, soil analysis subsequent to the flooding showed concentrations of 50 to 60 tons of salt per acre in some areas after the floodwaters had receded. How to remove this salt was the first consideration.

Another and more serious long-term problem was the damage to soil structure. Calcium predominates in most soils and has the effect of promoting granulation and the formation of a porous structure. During flooding the sodium in the sea water replaces most of the calcium, and the sodium clay thus formed has highly undesirable properties. It lacks the power of granulation and forms impervious sticky masses when wet, and rock-hard clods which fail to crumble when dry. To attempt to cultivate such land would only cause similar conditions at greater depth. Restoration would be prolonged and might take years.

There was no simple method of estimating how long the flooded land would be out of production, because there were too many variable factors, such as the length of time the land had been under water, rainfall, and the nature of the soil, whether sand, loam or clay. Heavy land reclaimed from the sea could be unfit to produce anything but grass for about five years. Many grasses have a fair power of recuperation after flooding, but the number of grazing days obtainable were bound to be reduced and, in the case of severe injury, the effects might last for three or four seasons. Once deposited in the soil the only way to get rid of the salt was to wash it out in the drainage water or so deep down into the soil that its presence would be harmless. So long as any free salt persisted in the ground, even washed down below the surface, with the coming of hot weather there was always the risk that it would rise again towards the surface within striking distance of the roots, not only poisoning the growing crop but constituting a menace to the recovering structure of the upper layers of the soil.

Another problem was that livestock in many areas depended

(*left*) *Aftermath of disaster:* Office staff at Shell–BP leave work. In the background is the flooded power house

Lincolnshire 1953 (below): A typical example of a reconstructed sea-wall. Mablethorpe area

on water from the field drains, now full of salt. In east Suffolk – as indeed in other localities – it was difficult to assess which was the more serious, the flooding of the arable land or the flooding of the marshes. Both arable and marsh represented serious losses, but the marshland presented an immediate problem. The coastal upland was all very light soil almost wholly utilised for arable, but practically every farmer had a herd of cows and some marshes had been heavily stocked. Now many farmers were left without a blade of grass to depend on. Also a large number of cattle from interior farms were accustomed to spend the summer on marsh grazings. In Essex the flooded grazings were for the most part out of action for some time after the disaster. Of the arable land under water, tests showed that nearly all was over the danger mark of flooding for crops. The situation was very serious.

But battered as were the agricultural lands fringing the coast, industrial premises situated along or near tidal frontages faced a no less difficult situation. Even though the water had receded from many of them on the ebb, it left in its wake sites choked with silt, sand and mud, wrecked plant and machinery, and merchandise either irreparably damaged or floating away and needing to be salvaged somehow. Neither could large industrial undertakings, unlike agriculture, look to the government for much tangible help. The Home Secretary told the House on 18 March 1953:

> In our view public limited liability companies fall into a different category both from individuals and personal businesses, and should not be compensated for losses which are capable of being recovered by insurance ... I am sure that the House will agree that it would not be right to expect the taxpayer or the ratepayer to subsidise big business which is well able to look after itself.

Nevertheless it was the responsibility of all the authorities concerned to do all that was humanely possible to prevent a repetition of the 1953 disaster.

Aftermath of disaster: Wreckage at the Purfleet industrial complex

The work of reinstatement of the tidal defences roughly divided itself into three stages: an emergency stopping of the breaches, secondly a consolidation of this work as a safeguard against possible storms coinciding with the equinoctial spring tides and, lastly, permanent repairs. Until the breaches had been closed and floodwater cleared from the land, production could not be resumed by the shattered industries along the coast, farmland sodden with salt water could not be recovered, and permanent remedial work to the sea-defence system could not be begun. The river boards concerned were confronted with a weighty task. For it was essential that work, which they might normally spread over anything from ten to fifteen years at their customary rate of progression, should be completed within six or seven months.

A high tide was predicted for mid-February, and a super-human effort to close the breaches was required if an even greater disaster were to be averted. It had to be borne in mind that there had been a considerable delay in the first flood during the breaking-up of the defences. This had retarded tidal penetration for a time, a factor which would be absent now, in the present collapsed state of the sea-walls coupled with denuded beaches and sand dunes. Spring tides would accompany the new moon of 14 February. The maximum height predicted for these tides, occurring two weeks nearer the March equinox, was almost 2ft (0·6m) higher than that which had been predicted for the tide at the end of January. The breaches must be sealed high enough and strong enough to hold these spring tides. So 14 February became an inexorable deadline.

Emergency measures, provided for after the 1949 floods, were brought into force at once. More than 30,000 men were soon at work. Over half of these came from the armed forces, both British and American; their help was magnificent and indispensable. Indeed it would be impossible to praise too highly the efforts of the servicemen, students, farmers, farm-workers, and volunteers from every walk of life, now called upon to grapple with the consequences of the disaster and to put things right. Civilians and servicemen worked side by side in biting wind and driving rain in a desperate attempt to rescue marooned people and livestock, to clear debris, repair the havoc, and block the breached defences with sandbags, stones and any other material to hand. Contractors were instructed to bring in all the equipment they could muster and to proceed to work day and night. The surge had particularly laid waste the Lincolnshire coast and here ten of the largest public works contracting firms in England were engaged to carry out the repair work. Sections of the 10 mile length of the most severely damaged sea defences were allotted to each firm, whilst about 4,000 troops and workmen, including lorry drivers from all parts of the country, were employed at various points.

Simultaneously the rescue and evacuation of livestock, arranging food for them and sorting out stray stock, was organised with impressive speed all along the coast. This was no easy task, particularly in areas like Foulness, where several miles of turbulent water separated rescuers from cattle

108

The flood victims: Stranded occupants are rescued from a flooded house in Whitstable, Kent

marooned on higher ground. The prompt and excellent salvage work organised by local farming committees prevented livestock losses being as heavy as at first feared. Farmers, stockmen and cattle-lorry drivers worked indefatigably all through the night of the flooding and throughout the following day under conditions of acute discomfort, sometimes of real danger. In the Lincolnshire marshes the hazards associated with driving lorries over the flooded roads were appalling. During the early stages of the flood only those with an intimate knowledge of the roads could move. Most of the fields were bounded by dykes and drains; hedges and ditches were rare. For long stretches there was nothing to show where the road ended and the roadside ditch or drain began; familiar landmarks were obliterated under a sullen sheet of water. Innumerable vehicles went off the road to be wholly or partially submerged.

The weather, too, was ominous. Everywhere along the coast

it was cold, with intermittent rain, drizzle, sleet and snow. Huge labour forces were isolated on the sea marshes, in conditions of intolerable misery, without shelter from the bitter north-east winds. One of the greatest problems of all the emergency works was access. Practically all the frontal walls were breached along many sections of the coast, and relatively few cross-walls existed. In many marsh areas cross-walls had at one time been common between first and second defence lines, dividing the area liable to flooding into compartments. These had served two useful purposes; firstly they controlled the extent of the flooding, and secondly they provided access to the walls under flood conditions for the purpose of effecting repairs. Unfortunately these had been allowed to decay and had even been demolished in some places, whilst little general effort had been made to extend the system elsewhere. Therefore, in all too many cases, there was no access whatsoever at a high level across the flooded marshes to the main seawalls. Because interminable miles of sagging, crumbling em-

The flood victims: Despite flood damage it is business as usual at F. W. Reynolds' shop at Herne Bay, Kent

bankment were unapproachable for close examination, the construction of suitable approach roads became a major part of
the emergency operations. Everything was delayed until they
could be provided. This partly explains the colossal requirements of civil and military labour which were found necessary
in the initial stages of the work.

The inconvenience and delay encountered by all and sundry
in many places defied description. In the case of the Breydon
wall that failed near Great Yarmouth the earliest repair works
were carried out by rowing sandbags out over the marshes to
the breaches in scores of small boats, whilst the business of
getting a dozen giant excavators, each weighing at least 30
tons, to the site over the soggy marshes proved a task of
almost insurmountable difficulty. Well might the subsequent
report of the Waverley Committee, established to enquire into
the causes of the disaster, call for improved access to the
defences as a first essential.

Even where approach roads did exist they were often
inadequate to the point of being useless. Those between
Tetney Haven and Saltfleet Haven in Lincolnshire were so
narrow that excavators on their way to the breaches had to be
conveyed along them one at a time. The top of the sea-wall
which constituted the sole access to sections of the Foulness
defences could be traversed only on foot. All tools, sandbags
and other essential equipment had to be carried along this
route from the main road, a distance of almost a mile.

There were other problems. In fact the whole enterprise
was beset by drawbacks of every description. In the vicinity of
Mablethorpe and Sutton the contractors had first to bulldoze
their way to the sites through several feet of sand, which
blocked all the roads adjacent to the coast. In some localities
there were no adequate outfalls to ensure the rapid evacuation
of floodwater. Consequently this had not been cleared away a
month after the storm, effectively delaying rehabilitation work.
And delay had at all costs to be avoided. On Wednesday, 4
February, the situation was so bad in the Lindsey area of

111

Lincolnshire that thirty-seven fire pumps were sent in by neighbouring fire authorities, and were employed in pumping operations at Skegness, Ingoldmells, Mablethorpe, Sutton, Chapel St Leonards and Barton-on-Humber until 9 February. On Tuesday, 10 February, the chaos was intensified by the failure of the mains water supply at Mablethorpe and Sutton. The entire force of water carriers in the County Fire Service had to be engaged until 17 February in running a continuous shuttle service to the nearest water point ten miles distant, in order to supply domestic and operational needs in the flooded area. Later a further fifty pumps had to be brought into the locality to speed up the task of dispersing the floodwater.

The actual task of closing the breaches was not a simple one. The vast size of the job – 15 million sandbags were used along the east coast – made its execution a feat of organisation. Moreover there were deadlines shorter even than the impending spring tides of mid-February. Every tidal breach had to be closed in the few hours between one high water and the next. As soon as the tide had ebbed low enough, a dam had to be hastily thrown up to a height sufficient to hold at the next high water. And once the neap tides were past it was a race against tides that were increasing steadily day by day. It was vital to close the breaches with all possible speed, because the longer the tide was free to ebb and flow through unchecked, the deeper would the breaches be scoured and the harder would be their final closure.

The work of closing the breaches was inevitably severely strained with each high tide, and the sandbagging was followed immediately by backing-up with soil. Some of the strengthening was done by driving temporary walls of steel sheet-piles. On exposed coasts, where there were concrete walls, stone and slag were used extensively for filling the gaps, and the material later formed an excellent filling for reconstructing the walls. At Sea Palling, one of the sites where the sand dunes had been breached by frontal attack, the ordinary breach-filling operation had to be supplemented by emergency measures to restore

112

the depleted beach and dunes. Temporary groynes, constructed of wire-netting and chestnut paling, were used to collect fresh material on the foreshore.

Along the Lincolnshire coast the main task was to construct at each gap an apron of steel piling and concrete, behind which hard-core had to be dumped in tremendous quantity to form a wall of considerable height and depth. The material had to be hauled from various slag heaps and quarries and dumped and bulldozed into position. Some of the filling came from as far afield as Derbyshire and Northamptonshire, but the largest single source of supply was Scunthorpe, in the north of the county. The magnitude of the task underlined the extreme seriousness of the catastrophe. At the peak of the operation about 2,500 lorries were engaged, each making two or three journeys daily. It was estimated that they were transporting 25,000 tons of material to the Lincolnshire breaches every 24 hours. Intermingled with this traffic was a steady stream of low-loaders and other special-type vehicles, bringing in engineering equipment, concrete and steel piling. About 420 miles (676km) of Lincolnshire roads were being used by the flood traffic.

Including the lorries themselves it was calculated that some 2 to 3 million tons travelled over the Lindsey roads during February. Unfortunately the narrow roads in the approach area had never been constructed with this completely abnormal weight of traffic in mind. Ice and snow constituted a further disability, hampering the operation. Heavy vehicles fractured water mains, and bridges and culverts had to be continually strengthened and repaired. The cost of reinstating the damage and wear was somewhere in the region of £150,000.

On 6 February the decision was taken to make an all-out effort to seal the Acre Gap adjacent to Sandilands. On completion of an emergency bank, a line of interlocking steel piling was to be driven across the breach to act as a coffer-dam for the permanent work to follow. Vast quantities of hard-core filling were rushed to the scene by an uninterrupted

Remedial operations at a notorious gap: Acre Gap, Lincolnshire –
emergency bank and steel-pile coffer-dam

flow of day and night traffic on the roads and railways. This
gigantic operation resulted in the extremities of the breach
being joined by 11 February. Thereafter Herculean efforts had
to be made to build up this immense wall to a level sufficient
to withstand the spring tides, now dangerously imminent. As the
labour force toiled on doggedly, in unspeakably wretched conditions, the race against time was intensifying. During the night
of 11–12 February snow fell, and snow ploughs were working
hard on the roads, particularly over the Lincolnshire Wolds,
across which poured an endless stream of traffic carrying
materials to the breaches, and for use in the emergency and
remedial works. At Sutton work was going on in 'fiendish
conditions' to raise the emergency wall another 2ft (0·6m). It
was bitterly cold, with a north-east wind driving snow.

Everywhere along the coast it was a similar story. More
than 130 men were toiling at the worst of the breaches in the
banks of the tidal Ouse at Magdalen Bend, striving to build up
a rampart of sandbags adequate to contain the swollen river
waters. The situation here was particularly ominous. On the

114

morning of 12 February the water at high tide had risen to within 2ft (0·6m) of the top of the gap. Within the next two days it could rise another 4ft (1·2m) or even higher. The work proceeded feverishly to keep pace with the inexorably rising tides. The cold was intense and snow flurries were sweeping the river. An eyewitness account described the scene on the night of 12 February:

> In the light of flood lamps, these men, most of them from the Royal Air Force, are filling up bag after bag with oozing waterlogged silt, and then lumping them into the gap. Backing them are five excavators, bogged down one behind another in the slushy earth. They pass great shovelfuls of soil forwards towards the gap, and their tall crane-like jibs seem to disappear out of the glare of the light into the black sky.

At Cley in north Norfolk the defences had 'held the first rising of the Springs, but at Wells ... the gaps are wide and fingers are crossed. Snettisham and Heacham, thanks to two dozen bulldozers and 400 R.A.F. still hold.' At Harwich, where disaster had struck with violent force,

> a north-east wind has been lifting up flurries of snow ... men ... have been toiling to close Harwich's main sea wall breach ... the last of some eighty thousand sandbags went on the emergency wall last night . . . the sandbag wall . . . stands about nine inches above the highest level the surge reached when it broke through the outer mud wall, for the present abandoned to the sea.

From Canvey Island, where light snow and sleet had been falling, little trouble was anticipated. A thousand men, knee-deep in gluey mud, had been

> working on the defence walls all day, two hundred are manning the wall now ... All the Canvey breaks are sealed ... plugged with mud and sandbags, and are so far holding. It is a tough job.

Boys from Ardale approved school at Grays, Essex, worked doggedly to close one of the breaches in the river Crouch defences near Canewdon:

> Conditions generally were appalling, and the mud was sometimes so deep that it came over the tops of the boys' gumboots. The weather was cold, with sleet and snow showers, and the mud was such that it was often easier to fill sandbags by hand rather than use a shovel . . . the boys worked resolutely and well.

Along the north Kent coast 4 million sandbags had been filled and stowed in the breaches. On the Isle of Sheppey convicts from the open prison toiled at the gaps alongside men from the Armed Forces. The US Air Force Base at Manston had been mobilised and hundreds of airmen rushed to Margate to help in rescue and repair work. A great fleet of lorries and bulldozers had been brought to the Northern Sea Wall, and material had been dug and conveyed from every conceivable source to stem the huge breaches. Formalities regarding acquisition had been rapidly overcome and in Kent too, by 12 February, the situation was being brought under some measure of control.

In the main the night passed without incident. Everywhere, strengthening and backing of breaches was going on. At some sites, by Friday the 13th, machines were moving out, their work done, That night progress reports from many regions suggested that the worst was over. Even at battered Purfleet most of the emergency operations had been successfully completed and industry was slowly grinding back into production. But here there was still no let-up in the efforts of the troops, who worked night and day to make the sandbag ramparts sheltering the factories and warehouses even higher and stronger.

A few breaches constituted persistent problems. In Lincolnshire many gaps could not be closed before the end of February owing to their size and difficulty of access. In

Norfolk and east Suffolk there were still major breaches unsealed at the spring tides of 14 February. These included the very large gaps torn in the defences at Wells, Breydon Water, Aldeburgh and Bawdsey. Breaches in the Breydon defences had not been properly sealed by 20 March. In Essex, even as late as 2 March, more than 10,000 acres still lay swamped in water. In Kent some exceptionally large gaps had not been sealed a month after the storm. In fact it was the end of March before all the east coast breaches had been closed. Then, although emergency work was still proceeding at many sites, plans for permanent reinstatement of the defences were rapidly taking shape, and permanent works were actually commencing all along the coast.

The immediate aim was to provide the same general standard of protection that had existed before the surge. This, taking account of the fact that the surge had practically laid waste the entire east coast from the Humber to the Thames, seemed completely inadequate. It was conceded however that for the defence of large industrial premises, areas of high population concentration and land of especial agricultural importance, it would almost certainly be desirable to provide a higher standard of protection. In this connection the tone of a memorandum of 27 February 1953, from the Ministry of Agriculture to the river boards concerned, is interesting considering the appalling circumstances:

> Even if it were desirable, it would not be practicable to provide such higher standard of protection all round the coastline before the end of September; and the question whether such higher standards should generally be provided is a matter for further consideration, having regard to the cost of the work and the value of the areas protected.

In fact where communities were living at risk, adequate protective measures were needed to safeguard them, disproportionate though the cost of such measures might be to the value of the property defended. The surge had proved that protection should not be sacrificed for economy. The real problem was to decide the measure and character of the defences that would be needed along the various lengths of coast to prevent a repetition of the disaster everywhere, not just in a few places considered to be of outstanding residential, industrial or agricultural importance. Meanwhile, on 19 February, the Home Secretary had outlined a proposal to set up a Committee of Inquiry into the whole circumstances of the disaster.

In general, restoration produced banks and walls that were thicker and stronger than their predecessors had been. In many places it was considered essential to raise the banks above their former height. On Canvey Island, where the loss of life had been catastrophic, the walls were given 3ft (0·9m) of freeboard above the storm surge level in the residential areas, and 2ft (0·6m) elsewhere. However, the difficulties confronting the engineer faced with raising a sea-wall were often formidable. In most places it was necessary to devise a means of giving additional height without adding appreciably to the weight of the structure. The subsoil weaknesses of some of the marsh areas was a problem. In the past it had been found hazardous to construct an embankment more than about 14ft (4·2m) above ground level, and even then slips had occurred in some instances. Where these conditions were apparent, also where there were obstructions by extensive industrial undertakings so that the wall could not be thickened to correspond with further heightening, it had evidently never been considered a matter of sufficient importance to design some form other than the heavy earthwork embankment. It was thought necessary now. Fortunately steel sheet-piling could be supplied quickly in large quantities, and was much used on restricted sites, particularly in front of industrial premises where there was insufficient space to broaden the banks at the base. The Essex River Board had this problem at Coryton, Thames Haven and Purfleet, and devised a means of using steel sheet-piling rather in the form of a fence. It had the advantage of lightness, speed of construction and a certain degree of flexibility. It would not crack if there were settlement. It might go slightly out of line but it would not give way. The defences at Canvey Island were clay walls, and here also the extra height was obtained by driving a fence of steel sheet-piles into the top of the bank.

For the future most clay banks everywhere along the coast were to be revetted with blockwork to the crest, particular attention being given to the strength of the blocks. The length of earth banks in Essex and Kent was shortened in a number of places by building dams across the creeks. Between Birchington and Reculver in Kent, Hunstanton and Wolferton in Norfolk, and in parts of Lincolnshire where the Roman Bank ran parallel with the coast, two lines of defences were established, the front line to act as a buffer and the rear bank as the main line should the front line fail. Along stretches of the coast between the Humber and the Wash and in parts of Norfolk and Kent where the sand dunes had been heavily damaged by the surge, new walls of reinforced concrete founded on steel piles were built. Apart from these general principles there was no uniform system of defence employed along the stricken coast. This was still left very much to each individual authority, and was dictated according to what local circumstances were supposed to be.

The Lincolnshire defences constructed after the surge, for the most part huge ramparts far removed from the earthen banks of earlier times, represented a considerable achievement. Along lengths where there was much property and life to protect, as at Mablethorpe and Sutton, the remedial works involved raising the sea-walls to a level which would give the fullest protection. In the main this was accomplished by piling the seaward toe and providing a stepped or sloping concrete outer face surmounted by a curved wave 'throwback' wall, behind which a concrete decking and a pitched inner slope protected the new wall from any scour. At Acre Gap and Sandilands similar standards were applied. Along the 5 mile

119

(8·0km) frontage from Sandilands to Chapel Point the Roman Bank was heightened and strengthened throughout its length. It temporarily became the effective coastline until land could be acquired and a new clay bank constructed on the line of the outer defences. This new bank was provided with a concrete toe-wall carried down into the clay, and with concrete partition walls to divide the seaward slope of the bank into 30ft (9·1m) wide bays. Hand-picked stone pitching was placed in these bays and grouted with a mixture of sand and bitumen, which is flexible, durable and gives resistance to impact and abrasion. Stone pitching itself is an ancient form of protection and consists of stone placed on the clay face of the wall, and keyed by wedge-shaped stones firmly driven into place. Revetment of this type is flexible and experience has shown it to be eminently satisfactory in almost every respect.

At Chapel Point the clay backing which had been washed away from the concrete defences was bulldozed back again. Immediately south of Chapel Point the existing sand dunes had been eroded and left dangerously thin. A clay bank was constructed along this length with stone groynes 30ft (9·1m) long and placed 30ft (9·1m) apart at its foot. At Trunch Lane, where a 600yd (548·6m) gap had been torn in the dunes, allowing the sea to burst through and inundate a large area as far as the main road over a mile inland, a stone wall 16ft (4·9m) high with a 25ft (7·6m) top width was erected. Between Vickers Point and Skegness the smashed defences were replaced by a continuous stone wall with an average height of 15ft (4·6m) and a top width of 24ft (7·3m). This was subsequently consolidated by concrete stepwork and a wave-wall where local conditions made it essential. Additionally the whole length was protected by steel interlocking foot-piling.

But these standards of protection were not invariably applied everywhere in Lincolnshire. In some areas the circumstances were not thought to merit it. The surge had inflicted appalling damage along the coastline between Tetney Haven and Saltfleet Haven, the sea having swept inland for a considerable distance with great force, drowning several people. Nevertheless, as the foreshore was wide along this frontage, the permanent remedial works were confined to the construction of higher and wider clay embankments faced with grass sods. Where possible sand was bulldozed back into the position of the former dunes. Brushwood was laid down on the beach to encourage the accumulation of sand. For the future it was decided to employ the two-bank system of defence along this section; it would be economical and effectively increase the safety of the locality. In extraordinary storm conditions both the force and period of the tide would be expended in the destruction of the outer bank and the inner bank would remain intact to cope with a reduced onslaught.

Further westwards along the south bank of the Humber, which had been overtopped over its entire length, the worst damage had occurred to the 12 miles (19·2km) of bank between East Halton and Grimsby. This section was raised to a height considered 'reasonable' in the circumstances, and widened to permit the passage of vehicles and excavators along the top. Concrete beams were carried down into the clay at the seaward foot of the bank and further concrete beams were placed on the seaward slopes at 30ft (9·1m) intervals. The latter formed separate bays which were filled with slag pitching and grouted with bitumenised sand. The crest was stoned. Between Grimsby and Tetney Haven the clay banks were heightened and widened. It was hoped that the very wide foreshore along this length of coast, coupled with the shelter from the full force of the waves afforded by Spurn Head, would obviate the need for more elaborate arrangements.

Meanwhile along the Norfolk coast remedial work was proceeding in a race to secure the coastline against the coming autumn and winter tides. To make the section between Wolferton and Hunstanton safe against high surges it was considered a viable proposition, in the long-term, to use the front line as a buffer and have an impregnable rear line, in preference to holding the front line by works of a really permanent character.

The cost of constructing concrete sea-walls along a distance exceeding 6 miles (9·7km) was thought to be unjustifiable, as there were no heavily populated or industrialised areas to the rear of the defences. Further inland, however, was very valuable agricultural land which demanded an adequate measure of protection. The shingle ridge which had formerly been relied on for much of the distance between Wolferton and Hunstanton, and which had been badly cut down by the storm, was still maintained at a minimum height and section but, due to the non-cohesive nature of the shingle, some displacement during on-shore gales was inevitable. Along this ridge the remains of several bungalows were removed, because they constituted an obstacle to the remedial operations and were, in any case, unsafe for habitation.

The concrete walls between Heacham and Hunstanton were reconstructed and strengthened as far as was practicable, particular attention being given to obtaining as much resistance to wave-impact pressure as was possible under the circum-

Remedial operations at a notorious gap: The sea-wall to close Hunstanton Gap, Norfolk, in process of construction

stances. Like the shingle ridge these were maintained to hold back all normal and high spring tides. At Hunstanton Gap the construction of a promenade 30ft (9·1m) wide was undertaken by the local council, galvanised at last into action by the extreme severity of the catastrophe. So far as the front line defences were concerned it was recognised that the shingle bank would almost certainly fail under extreme conditions and would have to be treated as a mobile defence line. But after improvements had been made to the Snettisham Bank, sited a short distance inland and now established as the main defence line of the area, both shingle bank and concrete defences became less important. In a crisis both would be expendable.

The Snettisham Bank was raised to a height of 4½ft (1·4m) above surge level, and strengthened. Preliminary work was commenced in June 1953 and completed by mid-September. During this time 7½ miles (12km) of bank received attention and 340,000 cu yd of earthwork was employed. In some places the seaward slope of the bank was concreted. It was thought that the protection it gave would be 'entirely effective', presumably under all conditions.

Along the tidal river Ouse the banks were heightened, in general a freeboard of 2ft (0·6m) above the surge level of January being provided. So far as King's Lynn was concerned it would be extremely expensive to give the town a very great degree of large-scale protection against high tidal surges, and difficult to carry it out, due to modifications which would have to be made to private property. For this reason, a compromise was adopted. A high degree of protection was given to residential areas, particularly to South Lynn where there was danger to life. A smaller degree of protection was outlined for other areas where danger to life was not involved and where potential damage to property was less. Accordingly the flood banks at West Lynn, a well populated area with some industry, were raised to a height of 3ft (0·9m) above the recent surge level. At places where local conditions precluded the use of banks, concrete walls were constructed, having a freeboard of 2ft (0·6m) above surge level.

On the east bank of the Ouse no such simple solution was possible. The level of the coping of the dock walls was 1½ft (0·5m), below surge level and that of the South and Boal Quays 3ft (0·9m) below. From the mouth of the river Nar to the Alexandra Dock there seemed no practical method of excluding a tide as high as that of 31 January. The most that could be done was to use flood walls and ramps to give protection up to dock coping level. Fortunately there was no threat to life in this part of the town and only relatively shallow flooding could occur. South of the river Nar was the lowest area in the town, where deaths had occurred due to the extreme suddenness of the flooding. Here the same defence standards were employed as for West Lynn.

Along the coastline between Hunstanton and Felixstowe there were many problems, not least the extent to which any large expenditure could be justified in the protection of relatively sparsely inhabited areas. In most cases remedial work involved making the tidal banks 1ft (0·3m) higher and 1ft (0·3m) wider at the crest; hence their freeboard in relation to the 1953 surge level was still marginal. However, it was considered desirable to rebuild the walls to a higher standard along some lengths. Those earthen banks with back slopes which had formerly been vertical were now given a slope with a gradient of 1:2. This constituted a decisive improvement. The existing ditches at the near rear of the banks were filled in and a new ditch cut further back on the marsh.

Along the length of coast protected by sand dunes the hills had been so cut away that their replacement was a virtual impossibility. On the section between Happisburgh and Winterton improvised groynes and brushwood were erected to build up the depleted beach. In the vicinity of Sea Palling two new lengths of sea-wall, totalling 16,650ft (5km), together with a number of groynes, were constructed. The longer of these two lengths extended from the existing Eccles wall, which had been badly damaged and had to be repaired, past Sea Palling and Waxham to a point where the sand hills still retained sufficient width and height after the storm to present a formidable barrier to the sea. The shorter length replaced the south end of the Horsey wall which had been demolished, and extended the wall southward to a point where the dunes were both wide and high. The new walls consisted of a stepped apron, surmounted by a curved parapet, with a steel sheet-piled toe and concrete bulkhead and a back wall to contain the filling necessary to construct the walls to the required height.

With the construction of these two lengths of wall the weakest section of the sand dunes received protection. Now that a fixed line of defence had at last been established over a large part of the area the aim was, in due course, to extend the sea-wall throughout the intervening 9,050ft (2·8km) length of sand dunes. In the meantime short groynes protected the gap between the two lengths of sea-wall, whilst a number of new groynes were planned with a view to stabilising the foreshore in the locality of Sea Palling and Horsey.

Further north along the coast there was a crop of problems of a different kind in evidence at Overstrand, where lack of proper drainage, absence of expansion joints, inadequate foundations and generally poor construction had been contributary causes of the failure, over a period, of the original defences. To cope with the problems a revetment was put in hand consisting of heavily braced timber piling. When completed it had the effect of accumulating beach material to a depth of 10ft (3·0m) and hence formed a secure protection to the cliff at the rear. The shattered sea-walls were enclosed in reinforced concrete with an apron and a steel sheet-piled toe. A series of steel groynes were also constructed. Drainage from the cliff at the rear was collected by means of a continuous shingle drain at the back of the wall, and piped through the walling. At Walcott nine 'holding' permeable steel groynes, 350ft (106·7m) long, were erected, and the coastline was eventually stabilised sufficiently by material accumulated by the groyning to permit the construction of a new sea-wall. The design of this followed roughly that of the successful one at Caister. A new sea-wall was also constructed at Kessingland, a little south of Lowestoft. New walling had in fact just been started at the time of the January storm, but had not proceeded far enough to prevent substantial losses of cliff.

In the various works at Walcott, Caister and Kessingland there was a strong family resemblance in design in the form of a substantial foundation, a sloping revetment, and a wave-throw-back wall. Permeable steel groynes were used in conjunction with most of the above works. The principles on which these groynes operate are simple. The sea containing suspended matter is calmed down and also the speed of the current, so allowing the suspended material to be deposited evenly over the beach. The groyne is zig-zag in formation in order to give stability. Construction is very basic, consisting of tubes, preferably galvanised, filled with fine concrete. These tubes can be readily lowered and are easily replaced if necessary.

Whilst the above works were proceeding in Norfolk and Suffolk, further south the Essex River Board too was planning and embarking on an extensive rebuilding programme. New standard heights were adopted for the sea-walls according to a combination of factors which included degree of exposure, type of foreshore, level of ground behind the walls, and size and kind of area to be given protection. Important industrial, agricultural and all heavily residential areas on the marshland were given special consideration. In effect this meant that along 75 miles (121km) of tidal defences improved standards of construction were to apply, with heights raised to 2ft (0·6m) above the 1953 surge level in the more vital agricultural areas, and 3ft (0·9m) above in the highly industrialised or heavily populated areas such as Canvey Island, Purfleet and Tilbury. The seaward faces of all clay walls were protected with a flexible, waterproof revetment, such as precast concrete blocks

Remedial operations in Kent: New sea-wall at Seasalter with groynes and dyke

grouted in bitumen, or with asphalt, up to crest level. A minimum crest width of 6ft (1·8m) was established.

Where building development, industrial premises or unstable conditions made improvement wholly in earthwork undesirable or costly, a light, flexible form of concrete or steel sheet-piled parapet construction was adopted. The provision of counter-walls was considered essential to provide access to the defences under flood conditions, as well as to limit the spread of salt-water flooding. In those places where creeks and inlets were dammed to shorten the defence line and reduce maintenance costs, the damming was done either with earth or with double rows of steel sheet-piling. This same expedient was applied in two places in Kent. Creeks which had outfalls, whether into the Thames or the Medway, were completely closed by damming them near their entrances. This saved the heightening of more than 10 miles (16km) of tidal walls which were too low to resist overtopping, and avoided heavy

Remedial operations in Kent: Beach re-charge scheme using sea-dredged shingle at Sheerness, Isle of Sheppey

expenditure on reconstruction and future maintenance costs.

A major consideration for the Kent authorities was the urgent need to strengthen the Grain sea-wall, defending the Anglo-Iranian Oil Company's refinery. This was heightened and reinforced, with secondary counter-walls running back to higher land to segregate the site. These earthen walls, where they confronted the sea, were paved with interlocking concrete blocks laid on the upper slope of the wall above existing ragstone pitching. For other places, where industrial expansion made it impossible to widen out the base of the wall sufficiently to obtain adequate height and stability, a light concrete structure was designed which could be superimposed on the existing sea-wall. Each section was a separate monolithic unit, 20ft (6·1m) long, with an expansion joint at each end of each unit. These had the advantage of quick construction. Also should undue settlement of the walls occur they were sufficiently rigid to be jacked up or repacked until the required level was again attained.

This expedient was also applied along the Thames estuary at the Erith sea-wall and at Callender's Cable Works. These had been badly flooded, with production halted for some time; it was essential to ensure that such a mishap did not recur in the future. The Graveney sea-wall along the Medway estuary, protecting agricultural properties, was also heightened and strengthened. As a precautionary measure it was equipped with a concrete parapet, as was the Seasalter sea-wall. The Isle of Sheppey walls were thickened and heightened by earthwork.

At Whitstable, where great trouble had been experienced from sea floods in the recent past, the council heightened the new wall by a further 3ft (0·9m); where possible a storm-surge barrier was constructed consisting of an elevated decking, level with the top of the wall, in conjunction with a curved parapet securely anchored to the sea-wall. It was impossible to adhere to this type of construction throughout the low-lying frontage of the town, in view of the number of yards and buildings jostling together along the waterfront; in some cases it proved necessary to provide a supplementary floodwall along the rear of the properties. The harbour area was encircled by a wall with the necessary ramps to provide access to the quay-sides for mobile cranes and lorries. The total cost was about £66,000 – a small price to pay for security against the dangers and damage of another flood.

Between Reculver and Birchington the Northern Sea Wall was strengthened by stepped concrete interlocking blocks on the seaward side, whilst the landward side was pitched with light concrete blocks. Timber groynes were constructed and the lower part of the slopes compartmented with timber piling and a steel sheet-piled toe. Meanwhile a new second line of defence was formed along the railway about ½ mile (0·8km) behind the wall. This was built of chalk, brought in by road and rail.

All along the east coast between the Humber and the Thames much had been accomplished in a short time. Millions of pounds had been spent on the new defences. The work had involved the movement of well over 10 million cubic yards of soil, the placing of 5 million blocks to face the sea-walls, and the use of more than 1,000 excavators and bulldozers. The emergency and permanent restoration work during the first year after the flood cost well over £20 million, the major share of this being borne by the taxpayer. In addition special grants had to be made to rid the soil from the salt affecting over 50,000 acres of land. Acreage payments for the rehabilitation of agricultural land, varying from £4 to £80 an acre, ran into hundreds of thousands of pounds. Gypsum was distributed free to farmers, at tremendous cost, to assist in eliminating salt from the soil. Apart from such primary considerations as loss of life, the expenses involved in repairing damage to the sea defences, agricultural land and industrial properties would appear to constitute a great incentive to prevent – by every possible means – a recurrence of such a large-scale catastrophe. However, to guard against every likely contingency no matter how hopefully remote, a flood warning system, based on information received from the Meteorological Office at Dunstable in Bedfordshire, was early devised and arranged to be operated continuously from mid-September to the end of April. It was hoped that this would act as a safeguard against loss of life.

The position in December 1953 was that, not only had the defences been restored but, in many places, improvements had been carried out. These improvements had been executed, generally speaking, with the object of making the defences strong enough to resist a tide of 1953 size. But in the light of all the evidence pointing to the possible fact that storm surges were becoming progressively worse, it is doubtful whether these improvements were completely adequate. The efficiency lag might still be present in some localities, as it had been for hundreds of years. There was still large scope for thought, research and experiment if there were to be any certainty that such a disaster would not recur in the future.

Chapter 7

LONDON ON
THE BRINK

As Londoners got out of bed on Saturday morning, 31 January, settling down to breakfast in bedsitting room, town flat or suburban villa, going about the hundred and one mundane tasks and occupations which formed the routine fabric of their daily lives, they were quite unaware of the speedily approaching disaster which they were to escape during the coming night by so disquietingly narrow a margin. The vagaries of wind and tide are not so noticeable in London's sheltered streets as they are on the exposed east coast, although their menace is not one whit smaller. In fact in London their menace, if less immediately apparent, is much greater, because a disaster in London comparable to that along the east coast would be far more vicious in its consequences, with a heavier death toll, involving a larger-scale evacuation of the homeless, and accompanied by greater social, industrial and commercial disruption and disablement.

With all this in view the staff of the Greater London Council's public health engineering department subsequently spelt out the plot of a disaster film which – according to the *Sunday Times* of 23 March 1975 – ran, briefly, as follows:

> A trough of low pressure moving east across the Atlantic pushes the North Sea towards its bottleneck at the Thames estuary. Heavy rain brings a swell of upland flow across Teddington Weir. The two coincide with a high tide, and the Thames bursts its inadequate banks.

131

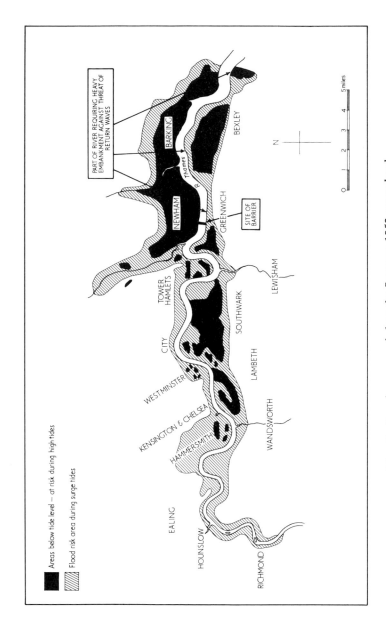

Map 5   London: areas below the January 1953 surge level

Legend:

■ Areas below tide level – at risk during high tides

▨ Flood risk area during surge tides

PART OF RIVER REQUIRING HEAVY EMBANKMENT AGAINST THREAT OF RETURN WAVES

SITE OF BARRIER

EALING

HOUNSLOW

RICHMOND

HAMMERSMITH

KENSINGTON & CHELSEA

WESTMINSTER

CITY

WANDSWORTH

LAMBETH

SOUTHWARK

LEWISHAM

TOWER HAMLETS

NEWHAM

BARKING

R. Thames

GREENWICH

BEXLEY

N

0   1   2   3   4   5 miles

At Westminster, a wall of water sweeps across the Embankment, surging into the House of Commons. The Tube from Westminster to the Temple becomes a watery grave for thousands. Nearly a million people over 60 square miles are quickly under water; motorists drown in their cars, pedestrians in the streets.

Power, gas and water supplies are knocked out, telephone and teleprinter services cut, and factories, shops and offices disabled. The whole nation is affected by the capital's paralysis. The cost runs into thousands of millions of pounds.

On the occasion of the 1953 floods, whilst others fought wind and tide through the weary hours of a long, black night, Londoners for the most part slept soundly in their beds. But would this always be so?

After the storm, whilst a great spate of remedial work was progressing to secure the east coast, the catastrophe there did not obscure the fact that central London, although it had escaped any flooding to speak of on this occasion, could not be overlooked in all this flurry of activity. In the past London had many times tottered on the brink of disaster and was in an extremely perilous situation now (Map 5). Large parts of the boroughs of Fulham (now part of Hammersmith), Wandsworth, Battersea (now part of Wandsworth), Lambeth, Stepney and Poplar (now part of Tower Hamlets), Greenwich and Westminster lay below the maximum level reached by the 1953 tide. Parts of Bermondsey (now part of Southwark), the Isle of Dogs (Tower Hamlets) and Woolwich (Greenwich) lay much below it. For it should never be forgotten that much of London, and most of its port facilities, are built on land reclaimed and held from the encroaching sea on a precarious tenure. Before the construction of over 300 miles (483km) of defences, great acreages on either side of the Thames were either flooded regularly by the high tides or else suffered periodic inundation at times of acute meteorological disturbance. So far as London has been concerned the Thames has figured in a dual role, representing at once an asset and a danger. London as a city and as a port owes much of its pre-eminence to the tidal river. On the other hand millions of tons of high-tide water pour up the channel twice daily. It is only the complex system of earthworks and embankments which in the past has stood between the adjacent low-lying areas and utter disaster.

The menace of Thames flooding has for long been an established feature of the major problems associated with the river. In 1236 the Thames was reported as overflowing 'and in the great Palace of Westminster men did row with wherries in the midst of the hall'. In 1242 the river frontage at Lambeth was flooded along a 6 mile (9·7km) stretch. When the Thames overflowed in 1507 the flooding of the marshes near London was extensive and severe. The situation was not helped by the fact that the maintenance of the tidal defences was abandoned largely to the capricious whims of individual landowners and tax dodging was prevalent, on this occasion 'divers that were assessed' for sea defence costs 'paying not their proportion'. According to William Dugdale the marshes would have been 'irrecoverably lost' had not the marsh bailiff and others 'laid down the money'.

There were other catastrophes. In September 1564 Holinshed reported how there 'arose great flouds in the river of Thames' and yet again in December 1565 which 'overwhelmed many persons'. In 1663, on 7 December, the diarist Samuel Pepys noted that 'there was last night the greatest tide that ever was remembered in England to have been in this river: all White Hall having been drowned.' The eighteenth century saw little improvement in the situation. On 31 December 1731 a high tide flooded the Tooley Street area of London just south of London Bridge; a vast quantity of merchandise in cellars and warehouses was destroyed. In 1736, Westminster, Southwark and adjacent areas were inundated. Tooley Street was again flooded by a high tide in 1747.

Some of the highest tides recorded in more recent times occurred in 1874, 1875 and 1881. The flood in January 1881 resulted from the coincidence of a spring tide with a gale from north-east in the North Sea, east in the Thames estuary, and south-east in the Channel, and with the break-up of a severe frost. The damage on this occasion was accentuated by floating ice. In November 1921 a tidal flood covered the tramlines on the Embankment and wharves in the City were under water. At Thames Haven the sea poured over the walls. The year 1928 saw a flood even more disastrous. It occurred on 7 January and every adverse element possible was present. Land floods caused by thawing snow and heavy rainfall were moving downriver, whilst a high spring tide driven by violent gales was advancing upstream. The water rose several feet above predicted height, and the river defences were overtopped or breached in the City, Southwark, Westminster, and as far west as Putney and Hammersmith. Because much of riverside London lies below spring-tide level a large amount of damage was inevitable. Fourteen people sleeping in basements were trapped by water rushing down the stairs, and drowned.

In London as elsewhere the entire flood problem was bedevilled by appalling administrative chaos. There was no co-ordination of action between the numerous authorities responsible for flood defences in the Thames estuary and along the tidal river. In some places no authority whatever was empowered to construct defences and, where the power existed, schemes were financed by a rating system so antiquated as to have been abandoned everywhere else because it was so demonstrably unsatisfactory. The Waverley Committee, reporting in 1954, dubbed the entire arrangements 'indefensible'. In central London, East Ham and West Ham the riparian owners were saddled with the full statutory responsibility for the heavy cost of building and maintaining defence works; works which, in reality, benefited relatively large areas extending well beyond the confines of strictly riparian localities. As the flood problem was so acute, requiring a massive expenditure of money to solve it, some other arrangements would obviously have to be sought, with the financial burden for tidal defence being spread more equitably through the general rating system.

When considering the flood problem in its many different aspects it has sometimes been argued that the removal of the old London Bridge in 1831 increased the liability of London to tidal floods. This bridge had been constructed on exceptionally solid lines in 1209. It was equipped with broad piers and with arches so narrow that nothing larger than a wherry could navigate through them. The eighteenth century, however, saw a sharp increase in the volume of Thames traffic, and to permit the easier passage of boats the centre pier was demolished. Even so the total space between the piers was considerably less ·than the space occupied by solid masonry. The water poured through the arches in cataracts, the difference in levels on either side of the bridge amounting sometimes to several feet. In fact so great was the force of the current that it was employed to drive the waterwheels which supplied London with water. The passage through the arches in a boat was equivalent to shooting rapids and there were several fatal accidents. But this unsatisfactory state of affairs, whilst representing a considerable setback to navigation, had one substantial compensating advantage. The tides advancing upriver expended a large part of their force and duration against the huge barrier of the bridge, so that upstream the tidal range was relatively small and the risk of serious flooding correspondingly less.

The immediate consequence of removing the old bridge, coupled with the subsequent dredging of the river, was to form a deep channel which facilitated tidal penetration. The average level of high water at Battersea and neighbouring parts of London rose more than a foot above that experienced before the removal of the bridge. The tidal flood problem became ever more acute and was probably further accentuated by the rebuilding of the Westminster and Blackfriars bridges in 1862 and 1869 respectively. The Thames embankments were constructed between 1869–74 in an effort to minimise the dangers. It is significant that the highest tide recorded before the removal of the old bridges was that of December 1663, when the tide rose at least 16½ft (5·0m) above the present ordnance datum, undoubtedly due to a highly exceptional meteorological disturbance. During the years from 1874 to 1882 this level was exceeded no fewer than six times, whilst the general level of high tide continued to show a steady increase, that of January 1928 exceeding all records. This increase was doubtless in some measure attributable to the decreased resistance to the tidal flow and the deepening of the channel after the demolition of the old bridges.

But there are other factors. Any analysis of the flood risk indicates that it is still increasing. Mean sea level in relation to the land is rising in south-east England, at Southend for example by over 1ft (0·3m) per century. Central London, on its bed of clay, is slowly sinking, and the mean tidal range, ie the difference between mean high and mean low water at London Bridge, is increasing by over 2ft (0·6m) every 100 years. This means, in effect, that high water is becoming higher and low water is becoming lower. At all events it is absolutely clear that high-tide levels in the Thames are getting higher in relation to the neighbouring land levels. But apart from land subsidence it also seems probable that this gradual rise in the highest tide levels may be partly due to the growth of Greater London, resulting in the replacement of large areas of porous soil by impervious surfaces. The construction of smooth, tarred road surfaces, off which water runs rapidly, might have some especial significance in this connection.

In January 1953 Central London was fortunate in that it escaped the worst consequences of the disaster. But it could not count indefinitely on this continued good fortune, and with its high population density, crowded buildings and underground railway system no chances could be taken. Even in 1953 the situation could have been completely disastrous had the right number of factors, working in adverse combination, been present. Had there been a greater volume of water flowing over Teddington Weir to augment the tidal waters already in the river, or had the maximum height of the surge occurred nearer the time of ordinary high water, the Thames would have been over into London. But the maximum surge did not occur at, or very near, high water, and the flow of land water was well below the winter average.

In 1953 London's defences coped on the whole, but by an uncomfortably narrow margin. Various tests carried out on the Port of London Authority's tidal model of the Thames showed that, if a high land-flood discharge of 20,000 cusecs at Teddington had coincided with the high water of January 1953, instead of the abnormally low discharge actually recorded, the maximum increase in level in London would have been about 9in (22·9cm). Since the level reached in 1953 only barely avoided causing serious flooding it became clear that even a small increase in freshwater flow would have resulted in a most serious situation. In view of the narrow margin of protection and the effects which a serious inundation of central London would have, it was important that action to minimise the risk should be taken without delay; for there was not a great deal of time to spare. According to investigations of the Greater London Council in 1970 about 55 square miles of London, with a population of 1,200,000 were below the maximum height reached by the 1953 surge. If London were severely hit it might take months to get the city functioning normally again, and the effect on the national economy would be disastrous. The cost, had said Sir Reg Goodwin, Chairman of the Greater London Council, could be at least £2,000 million, with injury and loss of life of 'unthinkable' proportions. That much was clear for the future. The losses caused by Thames tidal flooding in the past cannot, of course, be even approximately calculated, but total losses must have been colossal.

During recent years the vital need to protect London from disastrous flooding has been ever more clearly appreciated. This has led to an increasingly intensive search for a solution to replace the costly failures of the past; for efforts from earliest times to raise the river banks had been mostly in vain, because sooner or later they were overtopped by a flood even bigger than the one which had preceded it. Since 1953 Kent and Essex had spent large sums of public money in increasing the levels of their sea defences, but those nearer London were not completely adequate. To raise the Thames defences in the heart of London was no simple matter. It would entail not merely heightening existing structures, but would involve extensive rebuilding at tremendous cost of a complex business waterside, the re-laying of railway lines, dismantling and re-erecting gantries and cranes, and elevating warehouse floors and entrances. Some other expedient would have to be found.

There had been proposals for a barrage or dam across the Thames since 1811. Various sites had been suggested including Gallions Reach, Blackwall, Woolwich and London Bridge. One major group, with a fine disregard for navigation interests, wanted to dam the river entirely as far seaward as Gravesend. All proposals for a permanent barrage were opposed, first by the dock companies and afterwards by the Port of London Authority. A Thames bereft of its tides would effectively be deprived of the free motive power they provided for the river's heavy barge traffic. It was further argued that a permanent barrage would increase siltation, a sore point with the Port of London Authority, already faced with immense dredging bills. There is, of course, a sharp difference between a dam or barrage, which permanently shuts out the tides, and a barrier, which only excludes them on rare occasions. The general consensus of opinion came down heavily in favour of a barrier, assuming that one or other of these expedients proved essential to solve the Thames flood problem.

The Waverley Committee recommended for immediate investigation a scheme to erect a barrier in the Long Reach, just above Purfleet, and 19 miles (30·6km) below London Bridge. This structure would be equipped with gates which would normally be left open to leave the waterway clear. They would only be closed when an abnormal tide was known to be advancing on London. The committee thought the scheme a 'most interesting possibility' at the same time admitting that 'formidable engineering and financial considerations' were involved. It was hoped, however, that the matter would be investigated and a decision reached 'as quickly as possible'. That was in 1954.

In 1957 a great range of tests was carried out on the Port of London Authority's two tidal models, to study the possible effects of a barrier placed in the path of a travelling surge whose waters were compressed in an ever-narrowing estuary. The results of the research indicated that if the waterway were closed gradually over a space of about thirty minutes – starting four hours before the expected arrival of the peak of the surge – to the extent necessary to reduce the width of the waterway by 90 per cent, the maximum water levels at London Bridge would be lowered by just over 5ft (1·5m). Moreover with this degree of closure maximum water levels downstream would not be increased, so there need be no anxiety on that head, for example on Canvey Island or at Southend or Shoeburyness. Complete closure was considered unsatisfactory because it created too wide a margin of difference in the levels of water upstream and downstream of the barrier gates. But favourable as were the general conclusions ultimately arrived at, preliminary estimates of the huge cost deterred the enthusiasm of many. No action resulted.

But so acute were the potential dangers that the entire question was soon revived. In 1967 the Greater London Council began intensive investigations, and by January 1970 had got to the point of making a preliminary report. The 1970 conclusions embodied the proposal that a barrier should be so constructed that it could be altered to a permanent barrage if further investigation and events suggested this to be wise. Royal Assent to a Thames Barrier and Flood Prevention Bill came in August 1972, and the way was clear for a start to be made on the work. These preliminaries had not been finalised without numerous objections being lodged against the project. It was complained that the tidal area below the Thames

140

barrier would be left 'recklessly defenceless'. The fact that serious tidal flooding would put over a million people at risk, quite apart from the material threat to public and private property, did not deter a few individuals from questioning the advisability of constructing a barrier costing £75 million at 1970 prices.

Further problems were encountered over the choice of a site. More than a dozen were initially suggested, most of them being attended with drawbacks of one kind or another. The further upriver a site the less the shipping problem, but the greater became the complexity and cost of raising the downriver banks. Conversely, the further downriver the site, the less the bank-raising problem, but the likely interference with shipping was greater. Over 50 million tons of shipping per annum used the Port of London in the early 1970s, so the latter was a consideration of some moment.

The arguments against siting the barrier at the mouth of the estuary were legion, especially in view of the siltation problems that it would probably cause in the well known system of channels in the approach area. Moreover any barrier in the outer estuary, equipped with openings large enough not to hinder the passage of ships and to avoid siltation, would not protect the inland areas against a surge tide. In order to attenuate such a tide sufficiently, at least 85 per cent of the estuary mouth would need to be closed off.

The structural difficulties involved in gating large openings under these conditions seemed so complex that such a solution would require years of investigation. Even then there could be no guarantee that the end result would be successful. So when suitable chalk foundations were found at Woolwich during 1969 this seemed to be the timely answer to every problem. Navigationally the site is better than most. It is situated near the middle of a long, straight reach, and shipping surveys had shown that, in recent years, there had been a substantial decrease in the number of vessels passing through this particular straight. As it was anticipated that the barrier, at least during the early years after its completion, would be closed on average only a few times a year – and this included practice closures – its effects on the river traffic would be negligible.

The barrier was expected to be fully operational by about the late 1970s. Meanwhile, since this time was still a decade into the future, and since in the uncertain conditions prevailing almost any disaster could happen, the Greater London Council commenced interim flood protection measures by raising the river walls. In addition the Port of London Authority raised the height of protective walls at the docks, and the Lea Conservancy Catchment Board completed a small defence on Bow Creek.

For the barrier itself a type of gate was sought which would give unlimited headroom and a maximum span. The best answer appeared to be what is known as a rising-sector gate. Basically the rising-sector gate barrier is a series of separate movable gates built side-by-side across the river. Each gate is a segment of a circle held by a disc at each end, the whole rotating on bearings held between two piers which house the operating machinery and control apparatus. In the open position the gate lies flush in a curved concrete sill on the river bed, leaving a clear path for shipping through the opening between the piers. It is raised by means of a beam and link to its closed position in fifteen minutes should any dangerously high tide threaten. Owing to the limitations of structural steel and due to the possibility of a large differential head of water between one side of the gate and the other, the span of the biggest gate has had to be restricted to about 66yd (60·3m) width. However, there will be four main openings of this size, through which the largest of the ships using this part of the river will be able to pass. These four main gates are massive. Each is planned as a hollow steel-plated structure over 21yd

(opposite) London's new tidal defences: An aerial view of the Thames Barrier site, January 1976

(19·2m) high and weighing with counterweights about 2,946 tons (2,993 tonnes). There are two small rising-sector gates and two falling radial gates. The piers are over 71yd (65m) long by over 12yd (11m) wide, and are built in coffer-dams founded on the chalk.

The gates can be operated in three main ways. They can be raised at a late stage in a strong tidal surge, or raised at low tide, or raised only partially to allow the equivalent of a normal tide to pass upstream. The strong disadvantage associated with the first mode of operation is that a wave may be reflected down the estuary which, superimposed on the surge tide, would raise its effective height by more than 3ft (1·0m). Should the barrier be raised at low tide the surge level down-

London's new tidal defences: An artist's impression of the completed barrier

river would only be increased a few centimetres above its existing height. If the third method were adopted it would probably not increase the surge level downstream of the barrier at all, and might even lower it in places.

Although it is anticipated that initially this barrier will close once or twice each year to prevent flooding, by the year 2030 – due to continuing land subsidence – it will probably be necessary to close it about ten times each year. However, in order to exercise and maintain the barrier in good working order it will undoubtedly prove essential to close it more frequently than this. The times of practice closure will be chosen so as to interfere as little as possible with river traffic.

On the seaward side of the barrier the river defences are being raised to give the same level of protection as that given by the barrier itself. This has involved the river walls down to Southend on the north bank of the Thames and down to the Isle of Grain on the south side, and represents a project of immense scale. For although the £125 million barrier (1975 prices) is a most remarkable feat of engineering, in financial terms it represents a mere 50 per cent of the total investment. The heightening of the river banks constitutes the remainder. Therefore it would be a pity if the barrier were allowed to steal too much of the limelight from the equally important, albeit less spectacular, other half of the scheme.

The enormous cost of the enterprise – the £250 million budget seems likely to at least double while it is being built – is being met mainly out of central government funds and partly out of the revenues of the Greater London Council. There can be no doubt that the expenditure is justified. When the barrier is completed, by about 1981, Londoners will have an adequate defence from any future conceivable tidal surge for the first time in 2,000 years. But the project as it stands still cannot be said to embody a permanent solution. The life expectancy of the barrier and associated works – due to the continuing rise in mean sea level – is thought, in their existing form, to be limited to about sixty years.

Chapter 8

THE TIDAL DEFENCES, 1976

'All the art and science of sea defence engineering,' wrote Mr C. H. Dobbie in *The Municipal Journal* after the 1953 disaster, 'will have to be exercised to full capacity. There will be an opportunity for a comprehensive view to be taken of the defences and some very bold decisions will have to be made.' And certainly the immediate effect of the 1953 storm surge was to make the nation at large conscious of the danger of inundation and disaster from the sea. For the first time the problem was dealt with on a national basis and some monumental works were built at phenomenal speed. Moreover effort did not cease in 1953. Since then the sea-walls and banks defending long sections of the east coast of England have been extended, strengthened and repaired.

The Waverley Committee was appointed by the government to consider, amongst other things, the margin of safety for the sea defences, having regard to risks and costs. The committee's report was ultimately written on the basic assumption that the 1953 flood was to be the standard flood of all time. Its recommendations were based on this acceptance despite all the evidence to the contrary which suggested that there was a progressive increase in the surge-tide levels reached and in the frequency of such occurrences. The *Report,* in a singularly unfortunate paragraph, said:

> In considering the margin of safety for sea defences we have . . . had the protection of property mainly in mind. If there could have been a combination of all the known adverse factors, the water level reached in January 1953 would have been con-

siderably higher, possibly by several feet, than it was. The cost of affording protection against the worst possibilities would be colossal and we have ruled out any idea of being able to recommend measures designed to secure complete protection against every conceivable combination of surge and tide. Even the cost of protecting the entire coast against conditions like those of January last year would be prohibitive. To what then must the standard of defence be related? The natural and indeed inevitable course in these circumstances is to relate the standard of defence to the character and amount of the property to be protected.

Here it can only be said that where there are communities living at risk, however small or whatever the character of their property, adequate measures should be taken for their protection.

The standards of defence recommended by the committee were graded on a dangerously diminishing scale. A standard adequate against a 1953 type flood was established as the absolute maximum to be aimed at, and this only for areas with property of high value. Other localities were to fare even worse. For those not considered to be of overriding importance, either industrially, agriculturally or residentially, a somewhat lower standard was recommended, ie one which would have been thought adequate before the 1953 disaster. Where the value of the area to be protected was 'conspicuously below the general average', a standard lower than the very low standards which had prevailed before 1953 was envisaged. The committee thought that anyone requiring a higher standard 'may reasonably be expected to pay for it himself'. It was extremely fortunate that these extraordinary recommendations were made in conjunction with a proposal to organise a flood warning system, designed to prevent loss of life.

It was also fortunate that along some sections of the east coast the standards of protection actually adopted in relation to crest levels were well in advance of those advocated by the *Waverley Report*. This has been notably so in Kent, where many of the defences have been raised well above the margin

147

considered adequate to prevent severe overtopping by a surge of the height recorded along the coast in 1953. For example the Erith Sea Wall, forming part of the south bank of the river Thames, and protecting a mainly industrial area, has been heightened in some places by almost 4ft (1·2m) above the 1953 tide level. The Queenborough Wall at Sheerness, an exposed estuary wall protecting a built-up area, has been raised 4½ft (1·4m) above the highest level recorded in 1953. The Northern Sea Wall, a massive structure between Reculver and Birchington in Kent, facing north and directly confronting the open sea, has been given a freeboard in relation to 1953 surge level of 4½ft (1·4m) in some places, of 6½ft (2·0m) in others, and of 9¾ft (3·0m) in others, height in each instance being dictated by degree of exposure. The Nagden Sea Wall, also sited on the north Kent coast, has been raised 6½ft (2·0m) above the 1953 tide level.

Of the 267 miles (430km) of tidal defences now maintained by the Essex River Division of the Anglian Water Authority it is thought that 225 miles (362km) could withstand a surge of 1953 severity and also – according to site – a surge of from about 4in (10·0cm) to 3ft (0·9m) above 1953 level without being seriously overtopped. The crest levels of the remaining 42 miles (67·6km), which for the most part protect narrow belts of lower grade agricultural land, could cope with surges ranging from about 4in (10·0cm) to approximately 18in (45·7cm) below 1953 level.

Over much of the Suffolk and Norfolk coastline extending from Felixstowe to Hunstanton it has been impossible to ascertain what the freeboards of the sea-walls are, or to obtain any reassurance at all that the defences could withstand a really big surge. Despite the expenditure since 1953 of millions of pounds on the sea defences of much of this section, it would seem that considerable misgivings have been entertained about some of these, misgivings which – as will be seen – were to some extent justified by the events of early January 1976.

From Hunstanton round the shores of the Wash the sea-banks, after the 1953 surge, were strengthened and raised to a height of $4\frac{1}{2}$ft (1·4m) above surge level, and are considered capable of withstanding a similar occurrence. In Lincolnshire, the type of defence, and consequently defence levels, vary throughout the area, but it is generally thought that the existing defences here could also cope with a repetition of the 1953 surge-tide and wave conditions. It is considered probable that certain sections, such as the concrete walls reconstructed after the 1953 flood, and more certainly those sections reinforced with substantial dune defences, could contend with something in excess of 1953 levels. However, it has not been possible to identify such sections specifically, nor is it possible to say how much in excess of 1953 flood conditions they could withstand.

Research has been, and still is, vitally important in establishing efficient sea defences, and this was amply underlined by the *Waverley Report*. In 1954 the committee had stressed the need for an examination of many coastal problems, including the relative changes of land and sea levels still in progress, the generation of storm surges and their behaviour and frequency, and methods of improving natural and artificial defences. Two committees were subsequently established, one to advise on research designed to improve sea defences, and the other to advise on oceanographic and meteorological investigations.

The 1953 surge and the accompanying collapse of the defences had underlined with particular clarity the need to have a continuous record of changes taking place in the natural forces involved, such as waves, tides, currents and depths of water. In particular full-scale measurement of wave pressures was shown to be desirable, and it was emphasised that extension was needed in this work. Certainly sea defences could not be materially improved without this sort of information. Therefore whilst it was conceded shortly after the surge that measurement at sea involved difficult and cumbersome procedures and that new and easier methods were desirable, many sea-defence engineers emphasised that some improvements must be made whatever the difficulties.

However, arrangements for recording the continuous flow of water through the Straits of Dover after the 1953 flood were not particularly reassuring. It was done by means of measurements made on a 'spare' telephone cable from Dover to Calais 'kindly' lent by the Post Office for the purpose. The validity, as a measuring device, of a cable laid across the sea-bed is open to doubt. Any information obtained could scarcely have been of much use. Firstly any movement of the cable could not be appraised due to lack of any calibration. Secondly the movement of water on or just above the sea-bed differs greatly from its movement nearer the surface. Lastly the anchorage of the cable, presumably at both ends, would restrict its free movement.

Fortunately instrumentation developments since 1953, in relation to measurement at sea, have obviated the need for recourse to be had to such primitive methods. Now self-recording current meters exist, designed to measure and record the velocities and directions of currents and tidal streams. Readings can be recorded over a cycle in excess of six months, and at depths of 2,000ft (610m). There are also self-recording bottom-mounted wave and tide recorders with an operational depth of 100ft (30·5m), some specifically designed for conditions where the use of conventional types of tide gauge is not possible.

An outstanding difficulty is that coastal conditions are rarely stable and complete stability is always hard, often impossible, to achieve requiring, along some sections of the coast, frequent modification of the defence system. However, great as the problems are in this connection, it has in fact been the lack of long-term observation of basic data which has constituted the major setback in the successful design of past sea-defence works. Up to 1953 design had proceeded by hit-or-miss methods. Consequently unknown sums had been spent on inadequate protective measures, whereas a sufficient general knowledge of foreshore conditions would have facilitated the design of efficient structures with a minimum expenditure.

Finance is of course another reason, apart from safety, why definite and continuous information is essential before embarking on costly ventures which may prove useless. For example where heightening of sea-walls is concerned, the addition of even 1ft (0·3m) can incur a heavy added expenditure.

At the present time the Flood Protection Research Committee is actively engaged in work connected with all types of sea-defence problems. Hydrological investigations are being carried out by the research station at Wallingford, whilst International Conferences on Coastal Engineering are held from time to time. A great deal of work is done by the Beach Erosion Board in Washington and by the United States Council on Wave Research. Sufficient has been achieved to have a significant effect on sea defences, by enabling more efficient structures to be built in the light of the information obtained. It is assumed that those responsible for the east coast defences are availing themselves of all recent advances in this connection.

Sea-walls must be designed to withstand not normal but extreme tidal and wave conditions. Unless they can do this they are useless. The 1953 surge had demonstrated that failure of, or damage to, the works was not only caused by erosion and underscour. Failure by overtopping needs to be particularly guarded against, and if limited overtopping is allowed the walls should incorporate features which prevent collapse. There must be some doubt as to whether this has been done everywhere, for example at Walcott in Norfolk. Here the sea-wall, constructed on the heels of the 1953 disaster, collapsed in more than twelve places during the storm of 3 January 1976 under conditions which, though extreme, were not of 1953 severity. The wall was overtopped, which resulted in back-scour and subsequent breaching. In 1953, and during floods prior to 1953, most of the sea-walls had collapsed from identical causes.

Needless to say a vigorous maintenance policy is vital, otherwise even strong, well-designed defences will deteriorate to a point where they cease to be effective in a crisis. This applies not merely to concrete walls but to natural defences also. Everything possible should be done to conserve beaches, sand dunes and saltings, by groyning, fencing or by planting marine grasses or other suitable vegetation. But despite efforts in this direction there are beaches along the east coast which are suffering from marked denudation. At the time of writing (autumn 1976) the beach between Hunstanton and Heacham had dropped several feet below the toe of the sea-walls. This could well have unfortunate consequences for the frontal defences along this section of the coast. The dangers of breaching under these conditions are very much augmented because, when the beach is so low, the depth of water is correspondingly increased and consequently the volume and force of the waves.

In some places, however, considerable strides have been made in beach protection. There are cases where sea-dredged sand has been pumped ashore in an effort to conserve beaches. In a few areas shingle re-charge schemes have been carried out, using shingle either from points of the foreshore where shingle is accreting or from areas close inland. In Kent, at Sheerness on the Isle of Sheppey, even further advances have been made. Here about 230 cu yd (180,000 cu m) of sea-dredged shingle have recently been placed on the fore-shore over a length of 875yd (800m). A bank has been formed to withstand surge-tide conditions considerably in excess of those of 1953. Up to the time of writing this would seem to be the sole beach recharge scheme that has been carried out with sea-dredged shingle. Sand of course has a rather more limited value in dealing with foreshore erosion than has shingle, in so far as its resistance to wave impact is less and it is more easily washed out to sea.

Sea defence is so complex a matter that many think administration is another problem demanding urgent attention. As early as 1911 as we have seen, the civil engineer W. H. Wheeler had stressed the urgent need for a central sea-defence authority to establish certain basic standards of protection. He had deplored the practice of leaving so important a matter to the vagaries and whims of local endeavour, and to the frequently conflicting notions of many authorities. But despite the 1953 catastrophe, caused very largely by the existence of a weak and often archaic defence system, the idea still remained firmly entrenched that sea defence was a local affair, to be comprehended only by those with a detailed local knowledge. The administration of sea defence was therefore still left in the hands of authorities responsible for different sections of the coast, who were to decide on the strength of the defences in the light of local circumstances. No absolute standards were laid down. At the same time the Waverley Committee adopted the basic assumption that work locally based and devised should be paid for nationally out of central government funds, ie by the taxpayer. It was argued in some quarters that, after the 1953 flood disaster, there was every good reason to create a central authority which should try to see the east coast as a unit, and not as a piecemeal of isolated segments. The arguments in favour of both central and local control are legion; meanwhile sea defence still remains the immediate responsibility of various local bodies.

However, despite setbacks, discrepancies and difficulties, progress has been made in improving the sea defences of the east coast. Some of these met their first real test during the storm of 3 January 1976. So far as south Humberside and Lincolnshire were concerned the conditions were not quite identical with those of January 1953. In the Humber the tide was slightly higher than in 1953, but weakened progressively as it moved south. On the open Lincolnshire coast it reached 1953 levels but the wave action which had proved so disastrous in 1953 was less. Here wave heights reached 10ft (3·0m) as against at least 13ft (3·9m) in 1953. Moreover the wind in 1976 blew from the north-west and hence was directly off-shore, whilst in 1953 the wind had had a tendency to veer round more to the north-north-west. Further south, along the Norfolk coast, recordings at both King's Lynn and Wells indicated that the tide level was lower in 1976. It was almost 2ft (0·6m) down at Lynn and over 2ft (0·6m) down at Wells. Nevertheless the defences took a hard pounding. In the Great Ouse area alone, where the highest tide levels were almost 2ft (0·6m) below the 1953 maximum and the extreme conditions were of shorter duration, repair work ran into thousands of pounds. The damage to the coastline between Hunstanton and Felixstowe was even worse.

As in 1953 the storm tide occurred on a Saturday evening. The sea hammered the coastal defences from the Humber to Felixstowe, smashing chalets, cutting off three lifeboats and ripping large holes in concrete sea defences and promenades. Heavy south-west gales had veered to the dreaded north-west, so that the north Norfolk coastline was battered by direct on-shore winds. The flood warning system worked well; families living in vulnerable places along the coast had been evacuated several hours before high water and there was no loss of life. Fortunately the really high tidal surge expected in the wake of the gales never came. In direct contrast to 1953 conditions, when there occurred no significant ebb of the great surge tide before the next high water, high tide of 3 January 1976 ebbed away early and was followed by an extremely low tide whose peak was late in arriving. Hence a repetition of the 1953 disaster was averted. A coastguard at Walton-on-the-Naze, Essex, thought that 'if there had not been a let-up in the winds it might well have been a different story'. As it was communities suffered upheaval, inundation and evacuation, frequently returning to the litter of shattered homes. Events took a sufficiently serious turn to provide a timely warning.

At Hull the Humber and the river Hull overflowed and water swept into the streets, flooding houses, shops and offices. At Cleethorpes there was fearful havoc. The borough council's sea defences were breached in three places, the railway formation was washed away, about 50 houses were flooded, and a further 350 sustained varying degrees of damage.

Along the open Lincolnshire coast at Mablethorpe and Sutton a considerable volume of water passed over the defences into the adjoining streets, flooding many houses at or below street level. When the new defences here were designed following the 1953 disaster it was accepted that, in the event of a similar surge recurring, some overtopping of the defences would take place. Nevertheless this amount of overtopping, especially as it occurred under conditions less extreme than those of 1953, was considered unacceptable. It is disquieting to contemplate what might have happened had there been a bigger surge tide or heavier wave action. At the time of writing measures were being contemplated to reduce these effects. So far as the natural defences of Lincolnshire were concerned, the sea face of the sand hills along the entire coast between Cleethorpes and Skegness was very considerably eroded, as much as 16½ft (5·0m) being wiped off in some places. The sand hills immediately below Skegness were breached outright.

Further south the river Great Ouse at King's Lynn reached a height of 29ft (8·8m) at the peak of the tide. Some quays were flooded and parts of West Lynn. Nelson Street in one of the oldest parts of King's Lynn was swamped by water forced up from the drains, but overall flooding was not serious. The storm removed tons of sand from the dunes forming the sea-bank at Brancaster beach some twenty miles further round the coast, and adjacent land was flooded to a depth of several feet. Water poured over the top of the sea bank at Wells, and swept towards the quay, the car park and the quayside road. There had been a growing opinion in the town – now fully justified by events – that this bank needed heightening and strengthening. At Wells also large areas of sand dunes were swept away by the sea; in one place up to 21ft (6·4m) disappeared. The sea broke through at Blakeney and the shingle bank which – as in 1953 – still remained the sole defence of the village of Salthouse against inroads of the North Sea, was breached. The water flooded the marshes, swamping the coast road. On this occasion the only real casualties were the ornamental ducks kept in a pen on the marshes. At Sheringham the west end of the promenade collapsed; Cromer pier and promenade were damaged, as were the sea defences at Overstrand and Bacton. At Walcott the sea wall was breached in more than a dozen places, and the sea hurled blocks of concrete, each weighing more than a ton, across the coast road. About 150 homes were flooded, and Walcott reduced to a state bordering on near chaos. 'I moved in here a year ago and I wished I had never come', commented one resident, confronted by the wreck of his home after water, flowing over the sea-wall, had surged into the house.

Further along the coast three breaches in the north wall of Breydon Water sent torrents rushing through the gaps to cut the railway line between Norwich and Great Yarmouth. Water burst through weak points in the river Yare defence system, flooding parts of Yarmouth Southtown. The river Bure bank was breached and a hole torn behind the north end of the Caister sea-wall. It seems extraordinary that this wall, which in 1953 had been almost the only sea defence of any consequence to hold along the Norfolk coast, had been allowed to deteriorate to such an extent that it could not survive the less severe storm of 1976 without sustaining serious damage. Extensive repairs were now needed. At Lowestoft the sea broke through a gap in the defences causing some relatively minor inundation. Flooding on the railway line between Norwich and Lowestoft disrupted train services for a time. Water cascaded over the promenade at Felixstowe and families living in bungalows were forced to move into the upstairs rooms of adjacent houses.

Although the effects of the storm might have been many times more disastrous, events indicated the need for unceasing vigilance against the worst which the sea could do. For up to autumn 1977 there has been no test, comparable with 1953, of the new defences. And there remains the danger that the next great surge tide may be worse even than that of 1953.

Epilogue:

NO ENEMY BUT THE SEA

Serious as the 1953 disaster was, the combination of factors which produced it might have been even more catastrophic. The storm surge might have occurred when heavy rainfall had already swollen the rivers; it might have been superimposed upon spring tides with a higher predicted range; its peak might have coincided more closely with the predicted time of high water; the wind might have veered at the critical moment and increased wave action on the open coast.

In the past, since records have been kept, the maximum of the surge has never coincided with the moment of high tide; it has always been some hours before or after. Another feature is that no record exists of really high surges occurring at the time of the highest spring tides. They may have occurred at neap tides, at medium tides, even – as in 1953 – at low spring tides, but never has a high surge come at the time of a high astronomical tide. It is not clear whether this has been just a matter of fortunate chance, or whether there may be some physical reason. A form of counteraction between surge and tide has sometimes been suspected, but it is impossible to be sure.

In the absence of sufficient statistical evidence to indicate that a really big surge coinciding with a high spring tide is an impossibility in the future, there are no known reasons why combinations of surge and tide, more adverse than any hitherto recorded, should not occur. If a surge did coincide with the high water of a spring tide it might lead to an unprecedented disaster. Due to continued land subsidence calculations should

157

be made on the basis of higher and higher sea levels, of fiercer and fiercer storms, and of increasingly destructive waves. The situation leaves few grounds for complacency.

One point should be emphasised: there is absolutely no reliable guide to the probable date or magnitude of a future great flood. Meanwhile the possible low statistical frequency of disastrous combinations of storm and tide seems to have bred an attitude of undue optimism in some quarters. There has been – and is – considerable preoccupation with what is termed 'periodicity'; that is to say, an engineer designs his works on assumption of a flood occurring once in so many years, and indeed on the comfortable assumption that a great flood will not occur more than perhaps once in 200 years, or in the case of a really exceptional inundation perhaps once in a 1,000 years, and this in the teeth of all past evidence to the contrary. Such an optimistic pattern can scarcely be imposed on meteorological factors which, despite research, still contain a vast element of unpredictability. And even if it were possible to plot the probable statistical frequency of really big storm surges there are no methods, either precise or approximate, by which heights can be calculated years in advance. However, it is the current practice to relate defence levels to the calculated (statistical) return period for surge levels. Hence such terms as the 'thousand year flood', '250 year flood', 'five year flood' etc are bandied recklessly about, even though the very engineers who make such liberal use of these misleading terms are the first to admit that a 2,000-year, or even a 3,000-year flood cannot be guaranteed not to occur at any time.

For more than 100 years there have been progressive increases both in the highest levels reached in exceptional storms, and in the frequencies with which such levels occur. No part of these increases is due to any appreciable change in the tides themselves. Part of the increase is due to the continued land subsidence along the coasts of southern and eastern England. On the matter of recurrence the Waverley Committee published facts showing a startling increase in the frequency of very high sea levels. The records extend from 1820 to 1953, with a twenty-year gap from 1858 to 1877. From 1820 to 1896 the sea level at Sheerness never exceeded 13ft (3·8m) above datum; in the 39 years from 1896 to 1934 this level was exceeded twice; in the 20 years from 1934 to 1953 it was exceeded 4 times.

In this connection the ill-considered activity of developers along some sections of the coast ought to be seriously questioned. There is still a large amount of residential property being built on dangerously low-lying ground adjacent to the sea, even in those very areas which suffered appalling damage and loss of life during the 1953 floods. This is the more disquieting as, for the future, it seems unlikely that man can guard completely against so savage and unpredictable an enemy as the sea. It would be impossible to build sea defences which could be guaranteed against every possible eventuality. The most that can be done is to ensure that the money available for sea defence is not frittered away on costly, useless, ventures, but rather that it is spent on increasing the margin of safety, so that if a great surge does occur its full impact will be lessened. If the risk cannot be removed altogether it must be reduced by every means possible. Conditions like those existing in 1953 are fortunately comparatively rare, but they can and doubtless will recur. They have occurred many times in the past. Due to the great loss of life and widespread damage to property which followed in the wake of the 1953 surge there has been a tendency to regard it as a highly exceptional event. Previous storms have been just as severe, but because the number of people inhabiting the reclaimed salt marshes or tidal flats was relatively negligible, the devastation produced was correspondingly less.

The restoration of the pre-1953 status quo, even raising the defences to a height and strength capable of withstanding 1953 surge levels, or levels marginally in excess of them, should never be the sole or most desirable end. Whilst there is every reason to hope that a storm worse than that of January

1953 will not occur for many years, there is always the possibility that meteorological and tidal conditions may combine any winter to produce, out of the vast wastes of the north Atlantic, a great surge tide, more disastrous than any of its predecessors.

APPENDIX

The Storm Track – 29 January to 1 February 1953

TIME	PLACE	EVENTS
Thursday, 29 Jan Morning	North Atlantic between Iceland and the Azores	An almost stationary depression identified
Afternoon	North Atlantic	Depression heading north-east, then east-north-east deepening
Night	North Atlantic	Depression advancing towards Scotland, pressure falling at centre
Friday, 30 Jan 6am	North Atlantic	Depression still advancing towards Scotland – pressure at centre now falling below normal
Afternoon	North Atlantic	West-north-westerly winds driving water from Atlantic towards North Sea
Night	North Atlantic/North Sea	Depression advancing into North Sea. Wind veering to north-west. Severe gales reported in Hebrides. The Clan Line Steamer *Clan MacQuarrie* driven aground off the Butt of Lewis
Saturday, 31 Jan 6am	Orkneys	Pressure at centre of depression now falling to well below normal
9.30–10.30am		Winds of 90mph with over 125mph gusts recorded. Mean wind speed Force 11 (Storm)
11am–noon	Aberdeen	Mean wind speed Force 10 (Whole gale) with over 80mph gusts. Thousands of acres of forest area blown down

TIME	PLACE	EVENTS
About 2pm	Outer Hebrides	The Fleetwood trawler *Michael Griffiths*, with her entire crew of 15, sank
About 2pm	Irish Sea	Mountainous seas. Blizzards of snow and sleet. MV *Princess Victoria* sank, with loss of 132 lives
2.10pm	Aberdeen	High water rose 2¼ft (0·6m) above predicted level
3.20pm	Leith	High water almost 2ft (0·6m) above predicted level
3.30pm	River Tees	Water beginning to overflow banks
5.25pm	Sandilands, Lincs	Sea broke through sandhills. Flooding beginning to occur along much of Lincolnshire coast
7.10pm	Mablethorpe, Lincs	Defences opposite police station burst, flooding town centre several feet deep; 6,000 people evacuated from Mablethorpe–Sutton-on-Sea area. Death toll: 16. Skegness area also flooded. Death toll: 20
7.27pm	Hunstanton–Heacham–King's Lynn, Norfolk coast	Hunstanton to King's Lynn train halted by floodwater – forced back to Hunstanton
7.40pm		River defences overwhelmed at King's Lynn. People trapped in houses in low-lying parts of town. Death toll: 15. Most bungalows between Hunstanton and King's Lynn damaged or swept away. Death toll: 65
8pm	Sea Palling, Norfolk	Huge waves broke through sand dunes, engulfing much of village. Death toll: 7
8.30pm	Easington, East Riding of Yorkshire	Coastal and Humber defences breached. Damage to houses, shops, offices and industrial premises
10.13pm	Harwich, Essex	Tide started pouring over quay and into adjoining streets
10.18pm	Southend-on-Sea, Essex	The Norwegian tanker *Kosmos V* ran aground on Shoebury Sands in high winds and heavy seas
11pm	Gt Yarmouth, Norfolk	Breydon Water defences breached, inundating Yarmouth Southtown; 3,500 homes flooded. Large-scale evacuation. Death toll: 10

TIME	PLACE	EVENTS
Midnight	Isle of Sheppey, Kent	Sea broke in. Much of island, including Naval Dockyard, flooded. The frigate *Berkeley Castle* and the submarine *Sirdar* filed with water in the dock and capsized
	Whitstable, Kent	Water pouring over sea-wall into town
	Bramble Island, Essex	Explosives factory flooded. Night watchman drowned
Sunday, 1 Feb		
12.30am	Harwich, Essex	Water flowing into town from three directions. Deep flooding extending from quay to town centre; 1,200 homes flooded : 1,550 homeless. Death toll: 8
12.30am	Jaywick, Essex	Water pouring over sea front
	Canvey Island, Essex	Some sea defences overtopped. Flooding began in various parts of island as drainage dykes started to overflow
	Southend-on-Sea, Essex	Flooding occurring along entire front: 600 homes flooded; 34 homeless. Death toll: 2
12.40am	Tilbury	Water flowing over river Thames defences. 2,500 homes flooded; 6,102 homeless. Death toll: 1
12.45am	Shell Haven	Water pouring over river Thames defences, threatening oil refineries
12.48am	Isle of Grain, Kent	Sea flowing over sea-wall into Kent Oil Refinery
	Colchester, Essex	Water spilling over river Colne defences into industrial area round quay. Colchester to Clacton train put out of action
1–2am	Foulness Island, Essex	Completely engulfed; 368 homeless. Death toll: 3
	Gt Wakering, Essex	Housing estate of Nissen huts flooded. Death toll: 6
	Wallasea Island, Essex	Totally submerged. Death toll: 2
	Corringham Marshes, west of Canvey	Oil installations swamped
1.10am	Purfleet	Part of river Thames defences collapsed, flooding extensive industrial complex; 250 homeless

TIME	PLACE	EVENTS
1.10am	Sunken Marsh, Canvey	Sea burst through Tewkes Creek defences. Island completely flooded; 11,000 homeless. Death toll: 58
1.30am	Herne Bay, Kent	Water swept into town, flooding homes, shops and council offices
1.45am	Jaywick, Essex	Flooding occurring from rear across St Osyth marshes. Many homes washed away; 600 homeless. Deal toll: 35. Death toll at nearby Point Clear Bay: 2
1.55am	Canning Town, London borough of West Ham	Sea broke in; 150 homeless. Death toll: 1

BIBLIOGRAPHY

HISTORICAL BACKGROUND

Anon. *A true report of certain wonderfull overflowings of waters, now lately in Summerset-shire, Norfolke and other places of England* (1607)

Callis, R. *The Reading . . . Upon the Statute of 23 H.8. Cap. 5 of Sewers* (1647)

Camden, W. *Britannia* (1610), re-issued by David & Charles (1972)

Daly, A. A. *The History of Canvey Island* (1902)

Darby, H. C. *The Medieval Fenland* (Cambridge, 1940)

——. *The Draining of the Fens* (Cambridge, 1956)

——. *The Domesday Geography of Eastern England* (Cambridge, 1971)

Defoe, D. *The Storm* (London, 1704). Included in *The Novels and Miscellaneous Works of Daniel Defoe* (London, 1896)

Dugdale, W. *History of Imbanking and Drayning* (1662 and 1772)

Dymond, T. S. and Hughes, F. *Report on the injury to agricultural land on the coast of Essex by the inundation of sea water on November 29th 1897* (Chelmsford, 1899)

Flower, C. T. 'Public Works in Medieval Law', *Selden Society*, vol I (1915)

Garmonsway, G. N. (Ed) *The Anglo-Saxon Chronicle*, Everyman, London (1953)

Harris, L. E. *Vermuyden and the Fens* (1953)

Holinshed, R. *Chronicles of England, Scotlande, and Irelande* (1577), re-issued by the A.M.S., N.Y. (1967)

Knel, J. *A declaration of such tempestuous Fluddes, as hath been seen in divers places of England 1570* (London, 1571)

Lawrence, E. N. 'Floods of the Past', *Weather*, vol viii, no 3 (March 1953)

Lysons, D. *The Environs of London* (1796)

165

Perry, J. *An Account of the Stopping of Dagenham Breach* (London, 1721)

Richardson, H. G. 'Note on the Constitution and Records of Commissions of Sewers', *Report of Royal Commission on Public Records*, vol ii, pt ii (1914), p98

——. 'The Early History of Commissions of Sewers', *English Historical Review*, vol xxxiv (1919), p385

State Papers, Domestic Series (sixteenth and seventeenth centuries)

Thirsk, Joan *Fenland Farming in the Sixteenth Century*, Occasional Papers, University College of Leicester (1953)

Vancouver, C. *General View of the Agriculture of the County of Essex* (1795)

Webb, S. and B. *English Local Government: Statutory Authorities for Special Purposes* (1922)

Young, A. *General View of the Agriculture of the County of Norfolk* (1804)

——. *General View of the Agriculture of the County of Essex* (1813)

——. *General View of the Agriculture of the County of Lincolnshire* (1813)

GEOGRAPHICAL BACKGROUND

Green, C. 'Conflict of Land and Sea in East Anglia', *The Times* (14 March 1956)

Stamp, L. Dudley *Britain's Structure and Scenery* (Collins, 1971)

Steers, J. A. *The Coast of England and Wales* (Cambridge, 1960)

——. *The Sea Coast* (London, 1963)

White, W. *Eastern England, from the Thames to the Humber*, 2 vol (1865)

METEOROLOGY

Barnes, F. A. and King, C. A. M. 'Notes on the Causes of the Recent Tidal Inundations round the North Sea', *Survey* (University of Nottingham), vol III, no 2 (1953)

Bowden, K. F. 'Storm Surges in the North Sea', *Weather*, vol viii, no 3 (March 1953)

Brooks, C. E. P. and Glasspoole, J. *British Floods and Droughts* (London, 1928)

Corkan, H. 'The Levels in the North Sea associated with the Storm Disturbance of 8 January, 1949', *Philosophical Transactions of the Royal Society of London* (1950)

Dines, J. S. *Meteorological Conditions associated with High Tides in the Thames* (HMSO, 1929)

Douglas, C. K. M. 'Gale of January 31, 1953', *The Meteorological Magazine*, vol lxxxii, no 970 (April 1953)

Farquharson, W. I. 'Storm Surges on the East Coast of England', *Conference on the North Sea Floods*, Institution of Civil Engineers (1954)

Jensen, H. A. P. 'Tidal Inundations Past and Present', *Weather*, vol viii, nos 3 and 4 (March and April 1953)

Peters, S. P. 'Some Meteorological Aspects of North Sea Floods with Special Reference to February 1953', *Conference on the North Sea Floods* (1954)

Reynolds, G. 'Storm-Surge Research', *Weather*, vol viii, no 4 (April 1953)

Robinson, A. H. W. 'The Storm Surge of 31st January–1st February 1953', *Geography*, vol xxxviii, pt 3, no 181 (July 1953)

Rossiter, J. R. 'The North Sea Storm Surge of 31 January and 1 February 1953', *Philosophical Transactions of the Royal Society of London* (1954)

Welburn, H. 'Phenomena of Storm Surges', *East Anglian Magazine* (13 December 1955)

SEA DEFENCE

Bagnold, R. A. 'Interim Report on Wave-Pressure Research', *Journal of the Institution of Civil Engineers*, vol 12 (June 1939), p202

Crowther, G. Cubley 'Post-War Coast Protection Works along the South-East Coast of England, which have been undertaken by the Kent River Board', *Proceedings of the Institution of Civil Engineers*, vol II (1953)

Denny, D. F. 'Further Experiments on Wave Pressures', *Journal of the Institution of Civil Engineers*, vol 35 (February 1951), p330

Dobbie, C. II. 'Design of Sea Defence Works in Relation to Height of Tide and Degree of Exposure', *Conference on the North Sea Floods* (1954)

Duvivier, J. 'Coast Protection: Some Recent Works on the East Coast, 1942–52', *Proceedings of the Institution of Civil Engineers*, vol II (1953)

——. 'The Incidence of Storm Surges as a Factor in the Design of Coast Protection Works', *Conference on the North Sea Floods* (1954)

Mobbs, S. W. 'Sea Defence Works on a Sandy Eroding Coast with Scanty Littoral Drift', *Conference on the North Sea Floods* (1954)

Reports and Minutes of Evidence of the Royal Commission on Coast Erosion (1907–11)

Russell, R. C. H. *Coast Erosion and Defence*, Department of Scientific and Industrial Research (HMSO, 1960)

Thorn, R. B. and Simmons, J. C. F. *Sea Defence Works, Design, Construction and Emergency Works* (London, 1971)

Wheeler, W. H. *The Sea Coast* (1902)

THE EAST COAST FLOODS, 1953

Andersen, K. F. 'Gales and Gale Damage to Forests, with special reference to the effects of the storm of 31st January, 1953 in the North-East of Scotland', *Forestry*, vol xxvii, no 2 (1954)

Barnes, F. A. and King, C. A. M. 'The Lincolnshire Coastline and the 1953 Storm Flood', *Geography*, vol xxxviii, pt 3, no 181 (July 1953)

Cooling, L. F. and Marsland, A. 'Soil Mechanics Studies of Failures in the Sea Defence Banks of Essex and Kent', *Conference on the North Sea Floods* (1954)

Cotton, K. E. 'Flood Damage in Norfolk and Suffolk', *Conference on the North Sea Floods* (1954)

Crowther, G. C. 'Damage to the Kent Coastline, and Restoration Works', *Conference on the North Sea Floods* (1954)

Dobbie, C. H. 'The Flood Disaster Analysed', *The Municipal Journal*, no 3129 (1953), pxi

Doran, W. E. 'Sea Defences in the Wash and Estuary of the Great Ouse in Relation to the Tidal Surge of the 31st January, 1953', *Conference on the North Sea Floods* (1954)

Great Ouse River Division of the Anglian Water Authority: Flood correspondence, reports and memoranda 1953–69 relating to the storm surge and subsequent emergency and remedial operations. File relating to the *Waverley Report*

Grieve, Hilda *The Great Tide, The story of the 1953 flood disaster in Essex* (County Council of Essex, 1959)

Grove, A. T. 'The Sea Flood and the Coasts of Norfolk and Suffolk', *Geography*, vol xxxviii, pt 3 no 181 (July 1953)

Journal of the Board of Agriculture: 'The East Coast Floods', vol lix, no 12 (March 1953); 'The Treatment of Farm Land flooded by Sea Water', vol lx, no 1 (April 1953); 'County Reports on the East Coast Sea Floods', vol lx, no 1 (April 1953); 'East Coast Sea Defences', vol lx, no 8 (November 1953)

Macgregor, D. R. 'A Note on Canvey Island', *Geography*, vol viii, no 3 (March 1953)

Minutes of the Greater London Council, 3 February and 17 March 1953

Report of the Chief Constable. *The Lincolnshire Floods*
Reports of the Waverley Committee on Coastal Flooding: Interim Report (HMSO, July 1953); Final Report (HMSO, May 1954)
Robinson, D. N. 'The Failure of the Coastal Defences of East Lincolnshire', *Survey*, University of Nottingham, vol III, no 2 (1953)
Shell–BP News, no 66 (February 1953)
Shell Haven News, no cxxxii (February 1953)
Snell, E. L. 'Damage to the Essex Coastline, and Restoration Works', *Conference on the North Sea Floods* (1954)
Spalding, J. V. 'A General Survey of the Damage Done and Action Taken', *Conference on the North Sea Floods* (1954)
Steers, J. A. 'Lessons of the Flood Disaster', *Country Life* (February 1953)
——. 'The East Coast Floods, January 31–February 1 1953', *Geographical Journal*, vol cxix, pt 3 (September 1953)
Tomes, F. H. 'Damage and Remedial Operations on the Lincolnshire Coast', *Conference on the North Sea Floods* (1954)

THE FLOODS IN HOLLAND

Boerman, W. E. 'The Storm Floods in the Netherlands', *Geography*, vol xxxviii, pt 3, no 181 (July 1953)
Edwards, K. C. 'The Netherlands Floods. Some Further Aspects and Consequences', *Geography*, vol xxxviii, pt 3, no 181 (July 1953)
Meuwissen, P. G. 'The Flood Disaster in the Netherlands', *Journal of the Board of Agriculture*, vol lx, no 1 (April 1953)
Oughton, M. 'Letter from Zeeland', *Geography*, vol xxxviii, pt 3, no 181 (July 1953)

Newspaper Reports
Daily Telegraph, 2 February 1953
Kent Evening Post, 8–11 March 1977
News Chronicle, 2 February 1953
Nottingham Journal, 2 February 1953
Sheffield Telegraph, 2 February 1953
Wynn Jones, M. *Deadline Disaster. A Newspaper History* (David & Charles, 1976)
Yarmouth Independent, 6 and 20 February 1953
Yarmouth Mercury, 6 February 1953

THE THAMES FLOOD PROBLEM

Doodson, A. T. 'Report on Thames Floods', Meteorological Office, *Geophysical Memoirs*, vol v, no 47 (HMSO, 1929)

Holden, A. 'How London could drown', *Sunday Times* (23 March 1975)

Reina, P. 'Thames Flood Protection. River bank raising works to accompany the Thames Barrier', *New Civil Engineer* (15 August 1974)

'Surge Dam Tests to save London from Floods', *Daily Telegraph* (28 December 1956)

Thames Flood Defences (Greater London Council, 1974)

Thames Flood Protection. Plans and progress on the Barrier and associated defences up to Autumn 1974 (Dock and Harbour Authority, September 1974)

ACKNOWLEDGEMENTS

My first thanks are due to Mr R. Berkeley Thorn, Assistant Manager of the Kent River Division of the Southern Water Authority. As former Chief Design Engineer and Chief Engineer of the Kent River Authority Mr Thorn has for many years been responsible for over 150 miles of Kent tidal defences, now among the most impressive along the east coast. Concerning fundamental points of current sea-defence practice I have drawn heavily from his writings and his advice.

I am extremely grateful for the assistance of the following firms and institutions: the Anglian Water Authority, Bedford County Library, the Borough of Gt Yarmouth, BP Oil Ltd, Caister-on-Sea Parish Council, Cambridge University Library, Eastern Counties Newspapers Ltd, the Essex County Record Office, the Department of Public Health Engineering of the Greater London Council, the Greater London Record Office, the Institution of Civil Engineers, the Kent Record Office, the *Kent Messenger* group of companies, Lincoln Central Library, the Lincoln County Record Office, NBA (Controls) Ltd, Norfolk County Library, Rush & Tompkins (Civil Engineering) Ltd, Shell UK Oil, the Southern Water Authority, the *Sunday Times*, the Thames Water Authority, and West Norfolk Newspapers Ltd.

I would like to thank the following individuals who answered specific queries or helped in other ways: Mr J. S. Bissett and Mr D. I. Rollett, Managers respectively of the Great Ouse River Division and the Lincolnshire River Division of the Anglian Water Authority; Mr R. Crompton, formerly the

171

King's Lynn District Engineer of the Great Ouse River Authority; Mr George Hughes of Shell UK Oil at Shell Haven; John Lake, Field Engineer of the Rustrak Instrument Division of Gulton Europe Ltd; and Mr T. A. Valentine, formerly Manager of the King's Lynn Conservancy Board.

I am especially grateful to Mr David St John Thomas, Chairman of David & Charles Ltd, whose timely advice has considerably influenced the structure of the book in its final stages.

Several individuals and organisations have generously assisted me in the search for photographs. The Anglian Water Authority have provided plates 1–2, 11 and 12. I am grateful to BP Oil Ltd for permission to reproduce plates 5, 7–8. Plate 6 has been loaned by the *Farmers Weekly* and plates 15 and 16 by the Greater London Council. Plates 4 and 12 are reproduced by kind permission of the Kent River Division of the Southern Water Authority, and plates 3 and 13 have been loaned by Rush & Tompkins (Civil Engineering) Ltd. The *Kent Messenger* group of companies has provided plates 9 and 10.

The maps were drawn by Vic Welch.

INDEX

173